ISLAAMIC LEGAL RULINGS R~~~

HAJJ & 'U

VOLUME ONE

IBN BAAZ · AL-ALBAANEE · IBN 'UTHAYMEEN
IBN JIBREEN · AAL ASH-SHAYKH · IBN FOWZAAN
THE PERMANENT COMMITTEE FOR ISLAAMIC RESEARCH AND VERDICTS

TRANSLATED BY
ABU 'ABDULLAAH MOHAMMED AKHTAR CHAUDHRY

Islaamic Legal Rulings Related to Hajj & 'Umrah - Volume One
First Edition, Jumaada al-Awwal 1432 / April 2011

Copyright © Fatwa-Online Publishing 2011
www.fatwa-online.com | www.efatwa.com

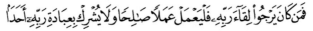

*"So whoever hopes for the Meeting with his Lord, let him work righteousness
and associate none as a partner in the worship of his Lord."*
The Noble Qur.aan - Soorah al-Kahf, Aayah 110

British Library Cataloguing in Publication Data
A catalogue record for this book is available from the British Library.
ISBN 9781907589027

Every effort has been made to fulfil requirements with regard to reproducing copyright
material. The Publisher will be glad to rectify any omissions at the earliest opportunity.

Compilation and Translation,   -   Abu 'Abdullaah Mohammed Akhtar Chaudhry
Cover Design, Typesetting and Layout by

Edited and Proofread by   -   SumayyahScott.com

Published by   -   Fatwa-Online Publishing
                           al-Madeenah an-Nabawiyyah
                           Saudi Arabia
                           eMail: publishing@fatwa-online.com

Distributed by   -   Darussalam International
                           146 Park Road
                           London NW8 7RG
                           United Kingdom
                           Tel: +44.20.8539.4885
                           Fax: +44.20.8539.4889
                           eMail: info@darussalam.com

بسم الله الرحمن الرحيم

Contents

Translator's Note

Indeed all praise is due to Allaah alone, who has allowed this book - **"Islaamic Legal Rulings Related to Hajj & 'Umrah" - Volume One**, to be made available in the English language. We pray to Him to grant favour upon this effort and to make it of benefit to both Muslims and non-Muslims. May Allaah guide us all to the 'right path', the path of the Prophet, Muhammad (*sal-Allaahu 'alayhe wa sallam*), and His Companions (*radhi-yAllaahu 'anhum*).

Firstly, whoever finds any mistake in the following work; either in the translation or typesetting, then please write to me (at my email address), indicating the mistake and its location, along with the correct translation.

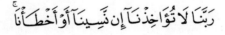

"Our Lord! Punish us not if we forget or fall into error..."[1]

---

1 The Noble Qur.aan - Soorah al-Baqarah, Aayah 286.

I thank all those who will point out any mistakes and correct the translation with the intention of seeking Allaah's Pleasure. Indeed, Allaah is Surety over what I say.

Additionally, I wish to thank all those involved in this work, in particular, the editorial team at SumayyahScott.com who agreed to undertake the mammoth task of editing and proofreading this book.

May Allaah (*Subhaanahu wa Ta'aala*) reward us and all of them with *al-Firdows al-A'laa*[2] - aameen.

May Allaah humble us all to make this effort pure; seeking His Face alone - certainly to Him is our return.

$$رَبَّنَا تَقَبَّلْ مِنَّا إِنَّكَ أَنتَ ٱلسَّمِيعُ ٱلْعَلِيمُ$$

"Our Lord accept from us, certainly you are the All-Hearing and All-Knowing."[3]

$$رَبَّنَا ٱغْفِرْ لِي وَلِوَٰلِدَيَّ وَلِلْمُؤْمِنِينَ يَوْمَ يَقُومُ ٱلْحِسَابُ$$

"Our Lord forgive me and my parents, and the believers on the Day when the reckoning will be established."[4]

---

2 al-Muntakhab min Musnad 'Abd ibn Humayd/182, al-Ahaadeeth al-Mukhtaarah aw al-Mustakhraj min al-Ahaadeeth al-Mukhtaarah mimmaa lam Yukharrijhu al-Bukhaaree wa Muslim fee Saheehayhimaa/394, Mawaarid ath-Thamaan ilaa Zawaa.id Ibn Hibbaan/2434: «*...and if you ask Allaah, then ask Him for al-Firdows al-A'laa*».

3 The Noble Qur.aan - Soorah al-Baqarah, Aayah 127.

4 The Noble Qur.aan - Soorah Ibraaheem, Aayah 41.

بِعَوْنِ اللهِ تَعَالَى،

وَ الْحَمْدُ لِلهِ الَّذِي بِنِعْمَتِهِ تَتِمُّ الصَّالِحَاتِ

*«With the assistance of Allaah the Most High, and
all Praise be to Allaah by whose favour good
works are accomplished»*[5]

Abu 'Abdullaah Mohammed Akhtar Chaudhry
eMail: abuabdullaah@fatwa-online.com
al-Madeenah an-Nabawiyyah, Saudi Arabia
al-Khamees 5 Rabee' ath-Thaanee, 1432 Hijree
Thursday 10 March, 2011

---

5 Sunan Ibn Maajah/3803, Musnad al-Bazzaar/533, Mu'jam Ibn al-'Arabee/1841, ad-Du'aa lit-Tabaraanee/1769, 'Amal al-Yawm wal-Laylah libnis-Sunnee/378, al-Mustadrak lil-Haakim/1840, al-Aadaab lil-Bayhaqee/718, al-Asmaa was-Sifaat lil-Bayhaqee/150, ad-Da'waat al-Kabeer lil-Bayhaqee/376, Sharhus-Sunnah lil-Baghawee/1380, Mu'jam Ibn 'Asaakir/419, Silsilatul-Ahaadeeth as-Saheehah lil-Albaanee/265, Saheeh al-Jaami' as-Sagheer lil-Albaanee/4640.

The Importance of Learning the Arabic Language

Whilst every effort has been made to render this translation from it's original Arabic source to English, one must appreciate the rich nature of the Arabic language and how difficult it can be to accurately capture the <u>true</u> essence of the Arabic text in *any* language. Allaah (*Subhaanahu wa Ta'aala*) says:

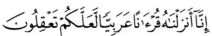

Verily, We have sent it down as an Arabic Qur.aan in order that you may understand.[1]

This book and any other book translated from Arabic should never allow the reader to become complacent and hold back from learning the Arabic language, ever! Rather, it should only serve a <u>temporary</u> purpose in assisting the student of knowledge on his way until he has attained his goal in having learnt the Arabic language.

When I began my Arabic language studies at the Islaamic University of

---

1 The Noble Qur.aan - Soorah Yoosuf, Aayah 2.

Madeenah back in 1993, I remember being interviewed by Dr. V. Abdur-Raheem[2] to assess the level of my Arabic knowledge so as to ascertain exactly which class he should enrol me into; It was then that I sought his advice by asking him the question every Arabic language student[3] asks – "O Shaykh! What is the best way to learn Arabic?", whereupon he advised: "Arabic is not learnt by simply memorising the grammatical rules, rather, Arabic is learnt through necessity..." – thereby guiding me to restrict my speech to the Arabic language as much as possible despite having just started my studies, wAllaahul-Musta'aan!

Poignantly, I recall a popular story our fellow Pakistani students at the

---

2 Author of the popular Duroos al-Lughatil-'Arabiyyah li-Ghayr an-Naatiqeen bihaa - Madeenah Arabic series of books, and at the time, Supervisor of the Institute of Arabic Language at the University. The Shaykh is currently the Supervisor of the Translation Department at the King Fahd Qur.aan Printing Complex in Madeenah.

3 My personal study notes prepared during my Arabic language studies at the Islaamic University of Madeenah and more study material – are all available for free download at http://www.fatwa-online.com

University narrate about *Shaykh* Ihsaan Ilaahi Zaheer[4]. When the young *Shaykh* arrived at the University as a student he was allocated a room in Building No.2 – which back then accommodated 6 students to a room. Upon discovering all his room mates were fellow Pakistanis he promptly made his way to the Dean of Student Accommodation and filed a complaint stressing that he had come to the University to learn the Arabic language and putting him in a room full of his fellow countrymen was detrimental to his efforts. He politely requested that he be placed in a room full of Arabs, whereupon his request was granted! *Subhaa-nAllaah!* Just listening to his Arabic audio lectures is testimony

---

4 Born on 31 May 1945. He studied in Jaami'ah Islaamiyyah Gujranwala and Jaami'ah Salafiyyah Faisalabad. He then started teaching and giving weekly khutbahs up until he left for Saudi Arabia. He studied at the Islaamic University of Madeenah and graduated from the Faculty of Sharee'ah. During his final year at the Islaamic University of Madeenah, Shaykh 'Abdul-'Azeez Ibn Baaz asked him to deliver lectures on the Ahmadiyyah – this is a very rare achievement. His book on the subject was then printed in Madeenah, but the young Shaykh wished to include in the book "Graduate of the Islaamic University of Madeenah" – before he had actually graduated! So he asked Shaykh Ibn Baaz, who was the Chancellor at the time and he agreed to it. The young Shaykh then asked Shaykh 'Ibn Baaz: "What if I fail my degree?" Shaykh Ibn Baaz answered: "I will close the University!" Upon graduating, he returned to Pakistan and pursued further education and received degree classifications of M.A.s in Arabic, Islaamic Studies, Urdu and Farsi.

He was taught by some of the major scholars of our time – namely: Shaykh Abdul Azeez Ibn Baaz, Shaykh Muhammad al-Ameen ash-Shanqeetee, Shaykh 'Abdul-Muhsin al-'Abbaad, Shaykh 'Atiyyah Muhammad Saalim, Shaykh Haafidh Muhammad Ghondalwee, Shaykh Abul-Barakaat Ahmad and Shaykh Muhammad Naasir-ud-Deen al-Albaanee.

He died on 30 March 1987, at the young age of 42; Shaykh 'Abdul-'Azeez Ibn Baaz led his funeral prayer in Riyadh, and the secondary prayer in al-Masjid an-Nabawee in Madeenah was attended by thousands. He was buried in the graveyard of al-Baqee' in Madeenah.

to his mastery of the language.

Imaam ash-Shaafi'ee said[5]: *'The language which Allaah favoured was the Arabic language as he revealed his Noble Book in this (Arabic) and he made this the language of the seal of the prophets Muhammad. And that is why we say that it is befitting for everyone who has the ability to learn Arabic – that they learn it, as it is the best language.'*

So, just imagine how much you have enjoyed reading a translated book; Now imagine how richer your experience would be if you were to read the original in Arabic!

Regarding the student of knowledge, *Shaykh* al-Albaanee was asked[6]: Is it obligatory upon a student of knowledge to learn and communicate in the Arabic language?

And the *Shaykh* responded: *Learning the Arabic language is an obligatory matter, as has been determined by the scholars, that:*

"If an obligatory act [A] requires you to undertake a secondary act [B] in order to fulfill the obligatory act [A], then that secondary act [B] becomes obligatory."

[That said], it is not possible for a student of knowledge to understand the Qur.aan and the Sunnah except by means of the Arabic language.

As for communicating in Arabic, then it is from the recommended acts, since there is no evidence to suggest its obligation.

---

5 Iqtidaa Siraatil-Mustaqeem - Volume 1, Page 521.

6 Fataawaa ash-Shaykh al-Albaanee fil-Madeenah wal-Imaaraat - Page 35.

Likewise, *Shaykh* 'Uthaymeen was asked[7]: It is apparent that many students of knowledge steer away from perfecting the rules of the Arabic language (grammar); Considering it's importance – what is your point of view?

And the *Shaykh* responded: *Yes, understanding the Arabic language is important, whether it be the rules of i'raab or the rules of balaaghah, all of these are important. However, based upon us being Arabs, and all Praise is for Allaah, then it is possible to learn without knowing the rules of the Arabic language. However, from that which is complete (and better) is for a person to learn the rules of the Arabic language. So, I encourage the learning of the Arabic language with all it's rules.*

Likewise, Shaykhul-Islaam Ibn Taymiyyah (*rahima-hullaah*) said[8]: *"It is known that Arabic is Fard 'alal-Kifaayah and the Salaf would discipline their children for making grammatical mistakes. Due to this, we are ordered, whether it be an obligation or a recommendation, to preserve the Arabic (grammatical) rules, and to correct the tongues that have deviated from the correct speech. By doing so, we preserve the methodology of understanding the Qur.aan and the Sunnah. We also preserve the following of the Arabs in their manner of (correct) speech. If people were left with their grammatical mistakes, this would be considered a great deficiency and despicable mistake."*

Shaykh Ibn 'Uthaymeen was also asked[9]: *Baara-kAllaahu Feekum*, is the fact that the *Qur.aan* was revealed in the Arabic language a justifica-

---

7 Kitaabul-'Ilm - Page 145, Question No.42.

8 Majmoo al-Fataawa - Volume 32, Page 252.

9 Fataawa Noor 'alad-Darb;
   Translated by Abu Abdul-Waahid Nadir Ahmad.

tion or an excuse for non-Arabs (for not acting upon it) due to it not being revealed in their language?

The *Shaykh* responded: *No, non-Arabs do not have an excuse or a justification in that the Qur.aan is not in their language; Rather it is upon them to learn the language of the Qur.aan, because if understanding the Book of Allaah or the Sunnah of the Messenger of Allaah (sal-Allaahu 'alayhe wa sallam) is dependant upon learning the Arabic language, then learning Arabic becomes waajib. This is because every action that has to be carried out, in order to be able to perform an obligation, acquires the ruling of being obligatory [or - All actions which if not performed first, an obligatory act cannot be performed, acquire the ruling of being obligatory (even if they are not an obligation within themselves, such as walking to the masjid for Salaatul Jamaa'ah (for men), since one cannot perform jamaa'ah in the masjid unless he walks there, the act of walking in order to get to the masjid becomes waajib upon that individual, and so on...)].*

Allaah (*Subhaanahu wa Ta'aala*) says:

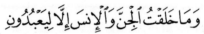

And I created not the jinn and mankind except that they should worship Me (Alone).[10]

In this *aayah*, Allaah (*Subhaanahu wa Ta'aala*) has clearly defined the purpose of our creation – our purpose in this life, and outlined the means which shall assist us upon this path in the Noble *Qur.aan* and the authentic *Sunnah* – both of which originate in the Arabic language.

---

10 The Noble Qur.aan - Soorah adh-Dhaariyaat, Aayah 56.

Considering this simple, yet essential fact, should provide us sufficient incentive to allocate time from our busy lives to learning Arabic which will subsequently open the doors to acquiring greater knowledge of this blessed religion of ours.

And what greater means to seeking knowledge can there be than to humble ourselves and sit at the feet of the inheritors[11] of the Prophets – the Scholars of *Ahlus-Sunnah* – and take directly fom them!

And as we take from them, we do so in order to worship our Lord upon sound knowledge, as Allaah (*Subhaanahu wa Ta'aala*) says:

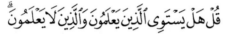

Say: "Are those who know equal to those who know not?"[12]

'So he who worships Allaah upon sound knowledge will find great delight and immense pleasure in his worship, as opposed to he who worships Allaah without sound knowledge.'[13] Therefore, as we pursue this noble path, let us recall the words of the Messenger of Allaah (*sal-Allaahu 'alayhe wa sallam*) who said in this regard:

«Whoever treads a path in search of knowledge,

---

11 Saheeh al-Bukhaaree, Sunan Abee Daawood/3641, Sunan at-Tirmidhee/2682, Sunan Ibn Maajah/223, Musnad Ibn Abee Shaybah/47, Musnad Ahmad/21715, Sunan ad-Daarimee/354, Saheeh Ibn Hibbaan/88: *«...and certainly, the Scholars are the inheritors of the Prophets...»*.

12 The Noble Qur.aan - Soorah az-Zumar, Aayah 9.

13 Shaykh Ibn 'Uthaymeen - Fat.h Dhil-Jalaali wal-Ikraam bi-Sharh Buloogh al-Maraam, Book of Purification - Pages 41-42.

Allaah will make easy for him the path to Paradise»[14]

...the <u>ultimate</u> reward!

I close my sincere advice with the case of a sister who strived and struggled to learn the Arabic language, despite the odds; Despite maintaining a 24-hour routine with her husband, both caring for their two terminally ill children with Batten's disease, Zakkee - 12 and Zahraa - 10, she *still* found time to pursue her passion for learning the Arabic language.

Her care shift would finish daily at midnight when I would visit her to teach her for up to an hour, and after I left, she would revise what I had taught her until 2am when she would go to sleep. She would be up again for the *Fajr* prayer and then resume her care shift at 8am.

My Sister, Umm Zakkee (*rahima-hAllaah*), died of breast cancer in the early hours of Saturday 16th *Ramadhaan* (1st December 2001) at the age of 35 years; Please remember her in your prayers.

May Allaah (*'Azza wa Jall*) permit her notes[15] to benefit all who seek to learn the Arabic language, and may He (*'Azza wa Jall*) cleanse my Sister

---

14 Saheeh Muslim/38, Sunan at-Tirmidhee/2646, Sunan Ibn Maajah/223, Musannaf Ibn Abee Shaybah/26117, Musnad Ahmad/7427, Musnad al-Bazzaar/9128.

15 "Umm Zakkee's personal study notes to Dr. V. 'Abdur-Raheem's ((Lessons in Arabic Language)) – Book 2; [as taught at the Islaamic University of Madeenah]" – available for free download at http://www.fatwa-online.com

of her sins and reward her with *al-Firdows al-A'laa*[16], *aameen*.

---

16 al-Muntakhab min Musnad 'Abd ibn Humayd/182, al-Ahaadeeth al-Mukhtaarah aw al-Mustakhraj min al-Ahaadeeth al-Mukhtaarah mimmaa lam Yukharrijhu al-Bukhaaree wa Muslim fee Saheehayhimaa/394, Mawaarid ath-Thamaan ilaa Zawaa.id Ibn Hibbaan/2434: «*...and if you ask Allaah, then ask Him for al-Firdows al-A'laa*».

Biography of
Shaykh 'Abdul-'Azeez ibn 'Abdullaah ibn Baaz
1909 - 1999

Abu 'Abdullaah Shaykh 'Abdul-'Azeez ibn 'Abdullaah ibn 'Abdur-Rahmaan Aal-Baaz was born in the city of Riyadh in *Dhul-Hijjah* 1330 A.H./1909 C.E.

He memorised the *Qur.aan* in his early age and then he acquired knowledge from many of the great scholars of the Kingdom. Some of his teachers were *Shaykh* Muhammad ibn 'Abdul-Lateef Aal-Shaykh, *Shaykh* Saalih ibn 'Abdul-'Azeez Aal-Shaykh and the eminent *Shaykh* Muhammad ibn Ibraaheem Aal-Shaykh who, in his time, was the *Muftee* of Saudi Arabia. *Shaykh* Ibn Baaz accompanied the eminent *Shaykh* and learned from him for about ten years. Thus he gained his religious education from the family of *Imaam* Muhammad ibn 'Abdul-Wahhaab.

Afterwards *Shaykh* Ibn Baaz was appointed as a Justice and he worked for fourteen years in the judiciary until he was deputed to the education faculty. He remained engaged in teaching for nine years at Riyadh Islaamic Law College, Riyadh Religious Institute. Then he was appointed Vice-Chancellor of the Islaamic University, al-Madeenah; but shortly afterwards, he was made the Chancellor with all the administrative powers. Later he was appointed President of the General Presidency of Islaamic

Research, Ifta, Call and Propagation, Kingdom of Saudi Arabia.

He held the position of Grand *Muftee* of Saudi Arabia, the Presidency of many Islaamic Committees and Councils, the prominent among these being: Senior Scholars Committee of the Kingdom, Permanent Committee for Islaamic Research and Verdicts, the Founding Committee of Muslim World League, World Supreme Council for Mosques, Islaamic Jurisprudence Assembly Makkah; and the member of the Supreme Council of the Islaamic University at al-Madeenah, and the Supreme Committee for Islaamic Propagation, until he passed away on Thursday 27 *Muharram* 1420 A.H./May 13 1999 C.E. May Allaah (*Subhaanahu wa Ta'aala*) have Mercy upon his soul, aameen.

The *Shaykh*'s official website: http://www.binbaz.org.sa

Biography of
Shaykh Muhammad Naasiruddeen al-Albaanee
1914 - 1999

He was born in the city of Ashkodera, then the capital of Albania in the year 1332 A.H./1914 C.E. into a poor family. His father al-Haaj Nooh Naj-jaatee al-Albaanee had completed *Sharee'ah* studies in Istanbul and re-turned a scholar to Albania. After Albania was taken over by atheism the family made *Hijrah* to Damascus. In Damascus *Shaykh* al-Albaanee com-pleted his initial education and was then taught the *Qur.aan*, *Tajweed*, sciences of Arabic language, fiqh of the *Hanafee madh.hab* and further branches of the Deen by various *Shaykh*s and friends of his father.

He also learnt from his father the art of clock and watch repair - and became highly skilled in that and famous for it and derived his earnings through it. He began to specialise in the field of *hadeeth* and its related sciences by the age of 20 - being influenced by articles in 'al-Manaar' magazine.

He began to work in this field by transcribing *al-Haafiz* al-Iraaqee's monumental 'alMughnee 'an-hamlil-Asfaar fil-Asfaar fee takhreej maa fil-Ihyaa minal-Akhbaar' and adding notes to it.

He delved further into the field of *hadeeth* and its various sciences despite discouragement from his father. Furthermore, the books he needed were not to be found in his father's library which was composed mainly of various works of *Hanafee* Fiqh - and since he could not afford many of the books he required he would borrow them from the famous library of Damascus - 'al-Maktabah adth-Dthaahiriyyah' or sometimes from book sellers.

He became engrossed with the science of *hadeeth* to the extent that he would sometimes close up his shop and remain in the library for up to twelve hours - breaking off his work only for prayer - he would not even leave to eat, but would take two light snacks with him.

Eventually the library authorities granted him a special room to himself for his study and his own key for access to the library before normal opening time. Often he would remain at work from early morning until after 'Ishaa. During this time he produced many useful works - many of which are still waiting to be printed.

The *Shaykh* faced much opposition in his efforts to promote *tawheed* and the *Sunnah* but he bore this with patient perseverance. He was encouraged by some of the noble *Shaykh*s of Damascus who urged him to continue, amongst them *Shaykh* Bahjatul Bayjaar, *Shaykh* 'Abdul-Fattaah -the imam, and Towfeeq al-Barzah - *rahima-humullaah*.

After some time he started giving two weekly classes attended by students of knowledge and university teachers - in which he taught various books of *'aqeedah, fiqh, usool* and *hadeeth* sciences.

He also began organised monthly journeys for *da'wah* to the various cities of Syria and then Jordan.

After a number of his works appeared in print the *Shaykh* was chosen to teach *hadeeth* in the new University in Madeenah, Saudi Arabia, for three years from 1381 to 1383H where he was also a member of the University board.

After this he returned to his former studies and work in 'al-Maktabah adth-Dthaahiriyyah' leaving his shop in the hands of one of his brothers.

He visited various countries for *da'wah* and lectures - amongst them Qatar, Egypt, Kuwait, the Emirates, Spain and England. He was forced to emigrate a number of times moving from Syria to Jordan, then Syria again, then Beirut, then the Emirates, then again to 'Ammaan, Jordan. His works - mainly in the field of *hadeeth* and its sciences number over 100.

His students are many and include many Shaykhs of the present day amongst them:
Shaykh Hamdee 'Abdul-Majeed, *Shaykh* Muhammad 'Eed 'Abbaasee, Dr. 'Umar Sulaymaan al-Ashqar, *Shaykh* Muhammad lbraheem Shaqrah, *Shaykh* Muqbil ibn Haadee al-Waadi'ee, *Shaykh* 'Alee Khushshaan, *Shaykh* Muhammad Jameel Zaynoo, *Shaykh* 'Abdur-Rahmaan Abdus-Samad, *Shaykh* 'Alee Hasan 'Abdul-Hameed al-Halabee, *Shaykh* Saleem al-Hilaalee.

The *Shaykh* passed away on Saturday 22 *Jumaadaa ath-Thaaniyah* 1420 A.H. / 2 October 1999 C.E. He was 87 years of age. May Allaah (*Subhaanahu wa Ta'aala*) have Mercy upon his soul, aameen.

The *Shaykh*'s official website: http://www.alalbany.net

Biography of
Shaykh Muhammad ibn Saalih al-'Uthaymeen
1929 - 2001

Abu 'Abdullaah Muhammad ibn Saalih ibn Muhammad ibn 'Uthaymeen at-Tameemee an-Najdee was born in the city of Unayzah, Qaseem Region on 27th *Ramadhaan* 1347 A.H./1926 C.E. in a famous religious family.

He received his education from many prominent scholars like *Shaykh* 'Abdur-Rahmaan as-Sa'dee, *Shaykh* Muhammad Ameen ash-Shanqeetee and *Shaykh* 'Abdul-'Azeez ibn Baaz.

When he entered into teaching, a great number of students from inside and outside Saudi Arabia benefited from him. He had his own unique style of interpretation and explanation of religious points. He was from among those scholars who served Islaam without any type of religious prejudice and kept themselves away from the limitations of blind-following. He was distinguished in his great exertion of effort in religious matters and analogical deductions which clearly prove the religious understanding he possessed, and the correct usage of the principles of religion, he adopted.

In giving religious verdicts, like *Shaykh* ibn Baaz, his *fataawa* were based on evidence from the *Qur.aan* and *Sunnah*. He had about fifty compilations to his credit. He taught Religious Fundamentals at the *Sharee'ah* Faculty of *Imaam* Muhammad ibn Sa'ood Islaamic University, Qaseem Branch. He was also a member of the Council of Senior Scholars of the Kingdom, and the *imaam* and *khateeb* of the big Mosque of Unayzah city.

The *Shaykh* passed away on Wednesday 15 *Shawwaal* 1421 A.H. / 10 January 2001 C.E. He was 74 years of age. May Allaah (*Subhaanahu wa Ta'aala*) have Mercy upon his soul, aameen.

The *Shaykh*'s official website: http://www.ibnothaimeen.com

31

Biography of
Shaykh Dr. 'Abdullaah ibn 'Abdur-Rahmaan Jibreen
1930 - 2009

He is the noble *Shaykh* Dr. 'Abdullaah Ibn 'Abdur-Rahmaan Jibreen.

He was born in Miz'al in the town of al-Quway'iyyah to the west of Riyadh in 1349 A.H./1930 C.E.

He studied with a number of scholars, amongst them his first *Shaykh* –
Abu Habeeb 'Abdul-'Azeez ash-Shushree, and also *Shaykh* Muhammad
Ibn Ibraaheem Aal ash-Shaykh, and *Shaykh* Ismaa'eel al-Ansaaree, and
his excellency the noble *Shaykh* 'Abdul-'Azeez Ibn Baaz.

In 1381 A.H./1962 C.E. he was appointed to teach various aspects of
the *Sharee'ah* at the Institute of Imaam ad-Da'wah. He then transferred
to the Faculty of *Sharee'ah*, specifically the department of *'aqeedah*. In
1402 A.H./1983 C.E. he was appointed a member of the Administration
of Islaamic Research.

In 1390 A.H./1971 C.E. he was awarded a Masters degree from the University of Imaam Muhammad in Riyadh. The title of his research paper
was 'Akhbaar al-Aahaad fil-Hadeeth an-Nabawee'. In 1407 A.H./ 1988
C.E. he was awarded a Doctorate with an grade of excellence, and that

was for his research paper entitled: 'Tahqeeq Kitaab az-Zarkashee 'alaa Mukhtasir al-Kharqee'.

He is a member of the General Presidency of Islaamic Research, Iftaa, Call and Propagation, Kingdom of Saudi Arabia. He also participates in various seminars and religious forums for the purpose of the propagation of the call to Islaam. He also delivers special lectures for the same cause. He has compiled many books and pamphlets on various Islaamic topics.

The *Shaykh* passed away on Monday 20 *Rajab* 1430 A.H. / 13 July 2009 C.E. He was 78 years of age. May Allaah (*Subhaanahu wa Ta'aala*) have Mercy upon his soul, aameen.

The *Shaykh*'s official website: http://www.ibn-jebreen.com

Biography of
Shaykh 'Abdul-'Azeez ibn 'Abdullaah Aal ash-Shaykh

He is the noble *Shaykh* 'Abdul-'Azeez Ibn 'Abdullaah Ibn Muhammad Ibn 'Abdul-Lateef Aal ash-Shaykh. He was born in Riyadh in 1362 A.H./1941 C.E., and since his birth he suffered from weak eyesight, until he lost his sight altogether in 1381 A.H./1960 C.E.

He began seeking knowledge by studying the Noble *Qur.aan* at *Masjid* Ahmad Ibn Sanaan, and memorised the Qur.aan when he was 12 years old. He then sought knowledge from some of the scholars in their gatherings. In 1375 A.H./1954 C.E. he transferred to the Imaam ad-Da'wah Institute where he graduated from the Faculty of *Sharee'ah* in 1383 A.H./1962 C.E., and he used to attend some of the gatherings of the scholars in their *masaajid*.

He began his active religous life after graduating from the Faculty of *Sharee'ah* in 1383 A.H./1962 C.E., whereafter he worked as a teacher at the Imaam ad-Da'wah al-'Ilmee Institute until 1392 A.H./1971 C.E. He then transferred to teaching at the Faculty of *Sharee'ah* (at the University of Imaam Muhammad) in Riyadh and continued there until 1412 A.H./1991 C.E.

He was then made a member of the Council of Senior Scholars in 1407 A.H./1986 C.E., whereafter he was made a member of the Permanent Committee for Islaamic Research and Verdicts, where he was appointed deputy to the grand muftee of the Kingdom (*Shaykh* 'Abdul-'Azeez Ibn Baaz) in 1416 A.H./1995 C.E.

He was the imaam for *Jumu'ah* prayers at the *Masjid* of Shaykh 'Abdullaah ibn 'Abdul-Lateef since 1390 A.H./1969 C.E., later transferring to being imaam at the Central Masjid of al-Imaam Turkee Ibn 'Abdullaah in 1412 A.H./1991 C.E. He became the *imaam* and *khateeb* at *Masjid* Namirah on the Day of 'Arafah in 1402 A.H./1981 C.E.

Whilst at the Faculty of *Sharee'ah* he used to supervise some university theses, and take part in theses discussions/debates.

Since 1414 A.H./1993 C.E. he has taken part in responding to questions on the radio program 'Noorun 'alad-Darb'.

He also used to hold lessons in the Central Masjid of al-Imaam Turkee Ibn 'Abdullaah. He takes part in seminars and lectures alongside his work in the field of *da'wah* in Riyadh and Taif.

The *Shaykh*'s official website: http://www.mufti.af.org.sa

Biography of
Shaykh Dr. Saalih ibn Fowzaan al-Fowzaan

He is the noble *Shaykh* Dr. Saalih ibn Fowzaan ibn 'Abdullaah from the family of Fowzaan from the people/tribe of ash-Shamaasiyyah.

He was born in 1354 A.H./1933 C.E. His father died when he was young so he was brought up by his family. He learnt the Noble *Qur.aan*, the basics of reading and writing with the imaam of the masjid of the town, who was a definitve reciter. He was the noble *Shaykh* Hamood Ibn Sulaymaan at-Talaal, who was later made a judge in the town of Dariyyah[1] in the region of Qaseem.

He later studied at the state school when it opened in ash-Shamaasiyyah in the year 1369 A.H./1948 C.E. He completed his studies at the Faysaliyyah school in Buraydah in the year 1371 A.H./1950 C.E. and was then appointed an infant school teacher. Then he joined the educational institute in Buraydah when it opened in the year 1373 A.H./1952 C.E., and graduated from there in the year 1377 A.H./1956 C.E. He then joined the Faculty of *Sharee'ah* (at the University of Imaam Muhammad) in Riyadh

---

1 Not to be mistaken with the town of Dar'iyyah in Riyadh.

36

and graduated from there 1381 A.H./1960 C.E. Thereafter he gained his Masters degree in *fiqh*, and later a Doctorate. from the same faculty, also specialising in *fiqh*.

After his graduation from the Faculty of *Sharee'ah*, he was appointed a teacher within the educational institute in Riyaadh, then transferred to teaching in the Faculty of *Sharee'ah*. Later, he transferred to teaching at the Department for Higher Studies within the Faculty of the Principles of the Religion (*usool ad-deen*). Then he transferred to teaching at the Supreme Court of Justice, where he was appointed the head. He then returned to teaching there after his period of headship came to an end. He was then made a member of the Permanent Committee for Islaamic Research and Verdicts, where he continues to this day.

The noble *Shaykh* is a member of the Council of Senior Scholars, and member of the Fiqh Committee in Makkah (part of ar-Raabitah), and member of the Committee for Supervision of the Callers in Hajj, whilst also presiding over membership of the Permanent Committee for Islaamic Research and Verdicts. He is also the *imaam*, *khateeb* and teacher at the Prince Mut'ib Ibn 'Abdul-'Azeez *masjid* in al-Malzar.

He also takes part in responding to questions on the radio program 'Noorun 'alad-Darb', as he also takes part in contributing to a number of Islaamic research publications at the Council for (Islaamic) Research, Studies, Theses and Fataawa which are then collated and published. The noble *Shaykh* also takes part in supervising a number of theses at the Masters degree and Doctorate level.

He has a number of students of knowledge who frequent his regular gatherings and lessons .

He himself studied at the hands of a number prominent scholars and jurists, the most notable of whom were:

The noble *Shaykh* 'Abdul-'Azeez ibn Baaz (*rahima-hullaah*);

The noble *Shaykh* 'Abdullaah ibn Humayd (*rahima-hullaah*);

The great *Shaykh* Muhammad al-Ameen ash-Shanqeetee (*rahima-hullaah*);

The noble *Shaykh* 'Abdur-Razzaaq 'Afeefee (*rahima-hullaah*);

The noble *Shaykh* Saalih Ibn 'Abdur-Rahmaan as-Sukaytee;

The noble *Shaykh* Saalih Ibn Ibraaheem al-Bulayhee;

The noble *Shaykh* Muhammad Ibn Subayyal;

The noble *Shaykh* 'Abdullaah Ibn Saalih al-Khulayfee;

The noble *Shaykh* Ibraaheem Ibn 'Ubayd al-'Abd al-Muhsin;

The noble *Shaykh* Saalih al-'Alee an-Naasir;

He also studied at the hands of a number of scholars from al-Azhar University (Egypt) who specialised in *hadeeth*, *tafseer* and Arabic language.

He has played a major role in calling to Allaah and teaching, giving *fatwa*, *khutbah*s and knowledgeable refutations.

His books number many, however the following are just a handful which include Sharh al-'Aqeedatul Waasitiyyah, al-irshaad ilas-Saheehil-I'tiqaad, al-Mulakhkhas al-Fiqh.hee, Foods and the Rulings regarding Slaughtering and Hunting, which is part of his Doctorate. They also include at-Tahqeeqaat al-Mardiyyah in inheritance which is part of his Masters degree. Further titles include Rulings relating to the Believing Women, and a refutation of Yoosuf Qaradaawi's book al-Halaal wal-Haraam.

The *Shaykh*'s official website: http://www.alfawzan.ws

The Permanent Committee
for Islaamic Research and Verdicts

A Royal Decree, number 137/1 and dated 08/07/1391 A.H. / (29/08/1971 C.E.) was issued for the establishment of the Council of Senior Scholars. Whereby, under section four it mentions:

'The Permanent Committee has been left the task of selecting its members from amongst the members of the Council [of Senior Scholars] in accordance with the Royal Decree. Its aim is to prepare research papers ready for discussion amongst the Council [of Senior Scholars], and issue *fataawa* on individual issues. This is by responding to the *fatwa*-seeking public in areas of *'aqeedah*, *'ibaadah* and social issues. It will be called: 'The Permanent Committee for Islaamic Research and Verdicts' (al-Lajnah ad-Daa.imah lil-Buhooth al-'Ilmiyyah wal-Iftaa.)'

Further, it is mentioned in section eight of the attachment to the Royal Decree:

'No *fatwa* will be issued by the Permanent Committee until the majority of its members have absolute agreement concerning it. Such, that the number [of scholars] studying each *fatwa* is no less then three members [of the Committee]. And if there exists an equal voice [differing in opinion], then the decision of the Head [of the Committee] will take precedence.'

The current members of the Permanent Committee include:
Head: *Shaykh* 'Abdul 'Azeez Aal ash-Shaykh;
Deputy Head: *Shaykh* 'Abdullaah Ibn Ghudayyaan;
Member: *Shaykh* 'Abdullaah Ibn Qu'ood;
Member: *Shaykh* 'Abdullaah Ibn Munee';
Member: *Shaykh* Saalih Ibn Fowzaan.

Amongst the members who have passed away include:
Shaykh Ibraaheem Ibn Muhammad Aal ash-Shaykh;
Shaykh 'Abdul 'Azeez Ibn Baaz;
Shaykh 'Abdur-Razzaaq Ibn 'Afeefee;
Shaykh Bakar 'Abdullaah Abu Zayd.

From amongst the rules (applied) in forming the [Permanent] Committee was the importance attached to the majority view [of the Committee], and no doubt this gives each *fatwa* an element of knowledge-based strength, for certainly exchanging views simplifies [the task of] arriving at that which is correct. Noting therefore, the path which the Committee has taken is selecting the opinion(s) which are based upon *daleel* (proof) in addition to the *daleel* from the *Sunnah* being from authentic *ahaadeeth*. The Noble *Shaykh* 'Abdul 'Azeez Ibn Baaz has assisted in this issue from his (vast) knowledge of *hadeeth*. Likewise, as has *Shakyh* 'Abdur-Razzaaq Ibn 'Afeefee's [vast] knowledge of the various groups and differences in *'aqeedah* that we have today, added an element of knowledge-based strength to each *fatwa*.

Chapter One

The Obligation of both the Hajj and the 'Umrah and their Conditions

1. Husband does not allow me to go for Hajj

Question: I am a wealthy woman, and I suggested to my husband more than once about performing *hajj*, but without any reason, he continues to refuse to allow me to go for *hajj*. I do, however, have an adult brother who wants to perform *hajj*, so can I [travel to] perform *hajj* with him if my husband does not permit me, or should I abandon [the idea of going for] *hajj* and remain at home in obedience to my husband. Please provide us a legal ruling, and may Allaah reward you with good?[1]

Response: Since the [performance] of the *hajj* is obligatory promptly once all its conditions are met, and since this woman has the financial and physical ability in addition to having a *mahram* [to accompany her], then it is obligatory upon her to hasten in performing the *hajj*; And it is not permissible for her husband to prevent her without any [legally acceptable] reason.

---

1 Fataawa al-Hajj wal-'Umrah waz-Ziyaarah - Page 14.

And in this case, it is permissible for her [to travel] to perform the *hajj* with her brother even if her husband has not consented. This is because [the *hajj*] is an individual obligation, just like the individual obligation of the prayer and the fast; So the Right of Allaah takes precedence, and this husband [of hers] who prevents his wife from performing the obligatory *hajj* has no right [to do so] without [any legally acceptable] justification.

And Allaah is the Expounder of all success, and He is the One who Guides to the Right Path.

Shaykh 'Abdullaah ibn Jibreen

2. Made an oath to go for Hajj every year

Question: Before I had a job, I made an oath to Allaah that I would perform *hajj* every year. However, my circumstances have now changed. I have a job as a soldier, and my supervisor does not permit me to go for *hajj* every year; I request [your] guidance - am I liable for [any] sin or not?[2]

Response: If that which prevents you from sometimes going for *hajj* is a matter which is beyond your control, such that you are unable to overcome it, then there is no sin upon you [in not going for *hajj* when the situation is as such] as Allaah (*Subhaanahu wa Ta'aala*) says:

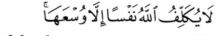

Allaah burdens not a person beyond his scope[3]

---

2 Fataawa al-Hajj wal-'Umrah waz-Ziyaarah - Page 18.

3 The Noble Qur.aan - Soorah al-Baqarah, Aayah 286.

And He (*Subhaanahu wa Ta'aala*) says:

مَا يُرِيدُ ٱللَّهُ لِيَجْعَلَ عَلَيْكُم مِّنْ حَرَجٍ

Allaah does not want to place you in difficulty[4]

And with Allaah lies all success and may Allaah send prayers and salutations upon our Prophet (*sal-Allaahu 'alayhe wa sallam*) and his family and his Companions.

The Permanent Committee for Islaamic Research and Verdicts

3. Makkan women performing Hajj without a Mahram

Question: Some women from Makkah travel to perform the *hajj* without their *mahram*, going in groups of women on public transport. So is this permissible?[5]

Response: That which is correct is that it is not permissible for a woman to perform the *hajj* without her *mahram*. Even if she was from the [resident] people of Makkah. That is because the distance between Makkah and 'Arafah is considered a journey according to the preponderant opinion [of the scholars], and this being the case, the people of Makkah would shorten their prayers along with the Prophet (*sal-Allaahu 'alayhe wa sallam*) throughout [their time at] the places[6] of the sacred rites.

Shaykh Muhammad ibn 'Uthaymeen

---

4 The Noble Qur.aan - Soorah al-Maa.idah, Aayah 6.

5 Fataawa al-Hajj wal-'Umrah - Page 11.

6 Minaa, 'Arafah and Muzdalifah.

43

4. Mother performed Hajj with other than her Mahram

Question: My mother, who is over 60 years of age, performed *hajj* with other than her *mahram*. Is her *hajj* valid or am I [now] required to perform *hajj* on her behalf, bearing in mind she has now died - may Allaah have Mercy upon her?[7]

Response: If a woman performed *hajj* with other than her *mahram*, then she is disobedient [to her Lord] and has incurred sin [by doing so]. This is because the Prophet (*sal-Allaahu 'alayhe wa sallam*) forbade the woman to travel without a *mahram* for *hajj* or other than *hajj*. As for the mother's *hajj* itself, then it is valid, *inshaa.-Allaah*. However, she has incurred sin and we hope Allaah forgives her [for this].

Shaykh Saalih ibn Fowzaan

5. Performed Hajj when I was ten years old

Question: I performed *hajj* when I was ten years old, and once again, when I was thirteen years old. So, do both of these *hajjs'* constitute the obligatory *hajj*?[8]

Response: The *hajjs'* as mentioned suffice the obligatory *hajj* if they were [performed] after you came of age; [That being] either by having a wet dream, or the appearance of pubic hair. This is because [both] the male and female come of age by either of these two occurrences, in addition to reaching the age of fifteen years. And in the case of women

---

7 al-Muntaqaa min Fataawa Ibn Fowzaan - Volume 3, Page 168, Fatwa No.253.

8 Fataawa al-Lajnah ad-Daa.imah lil-Buhooth al-'Ilmiyyah wal-Iftaa. - Volume 11, Page 23, Fatwa No.10938.

– beginning the menstrual cycle.

And with Allaah lies all success and may Allaah send prayers and saluta-tions upon our Prophet (*sal-Allaahu 'alayhe wa sallam*) and his family and his Companions.

The Permanent Committee for Islaamic Research and Verdicts

6. Performed Hajj whilst Pregnant

Question: A woman performed *hajj* whilst she was pregnant. When she returned from the *hajj*, her [unborn] child died. So, will she and her child be rewarded for that *hajj*?[9]

Response: Only the woman will be rewarded for the *hajj*. As for her child, then there is no *hajj* for him.

And with Allaah lies all success and may Allaah send prayers and saluta-tions upon our Prophet (*sal-Allaahu 'alayhe wa sallam*) and his family and his Companions.

The Permanent Committee for Islaamic Research and Verdicts

7. Performed Hajj with group of women and not Mahram

Question: A woman performed her obligatory [first] *hajj* without a *mah-ram*, and instead, with a group of pious and noble women. So has her

---

9 Fataawa al-Lajnah ad-Daa.imah lil-Buhooth al-'Ilmiyyah wal-Iftaa. - Volume 11, Page 16, Fatwa No.2177.

45

obligation [of performing *hajj*] now been fulfilled or not?[10]

Response: If the situation is as mentioned, then her *hajj* is valid, and her obligation [of performing *hajj*] has been fulfilled; However, she has incurred sin by travelling without her *mahram*, and she must [therefore] repent to Allaah and seek [His] forgiveness.

And with Allaah lies all success and may Allaah send prayers and salutations upon our Prophet (*sal-Allaahu 'alayhe wa sallam*) and his family and his Companions.

The Permanent Committee for Islaamic Research and Verdicts

8. Performed Hajj without Husband's Permission

Question: What is the ruling regarding a wife who leaves to perform the obligatory [first] *hajj* without her husband's permission?[11]

Response: The obligatory *hajj* is [only] obligatory if [all] its conditions are satisfied and [seeking] the permission of the husband is not from amongst them. It is not permissible for him to prevent her, rather, it is legislated for him to assist her in performing this obligation.

And with Allaah lies all success and may Allaah send prayers and salutations upon our Prophet (*sal-Allaahu 'alayhe wa sallam*) and his family and his Companions.

The Permanent Committee for Islaamic Research and Verdicts

---

10 Fataawa al-Lajnah ad-Daa.imah lil-Buhooth al-'Ilmiyyah wal-Iftaa. - Volume 11, Page 97, Question 1 of Fatwa No.9552.

11 Fataawa al-Lajnah ad-Daa.imah lil-Buhooth al-'Ilmiyyah wal-Iftaa. - Volume 11, Page 20, Fatwa No. 5866.

9. Performing Hajj every year

Question: A man is able to perform *hajj* every year, and some of the people have said to him [in doing so] he is causing harm and discomfort to the other pilgrims. So is this true?[12]

Response: That which is correct is the performance of *hajj* is legislated [for] every year. This is because the Prophet (*sal-Allaahu 'alayhe wa sallam*) encouraged it, as he said:

«...and the reward for an accepted hajj is nothing less than Paradise»[13]

However, if you fear the *fitnah* in regularly performing the *hajj* - that being seeing the women and [experiencing] the extreme crowding of the men and the women - whilst you have already performed your [first] obligatory *hajj*, then it can be said abstaining from performing the *hajj* is better; And [in doing so, you can] donate the funds allocated for the *hajj* to charitable causes. That is because 'averting evil and corruption takes precedence over procuring benefits'[14].

As for the man who performs *hajj* with calm and caution and with noble manners, then it is possible for the people to benefit from his knowl-

---

12 Fataawa al-Hajj wal-'Umrah - Page 9.

13 Saheeh al-Bukhaaree/1773, Saheeh Muslim/437, Sunan at-Tirmidhee/933, Sunan an-Nasaa.ee/2629, Sunan Ibn Maajah/2888, Musnad Abee Daawood at-Tiyaalisee/2547, Musannaf 'Abdir-Razzaaq/8799, Musnad al-Humaydee/1032, Musannaf Ibn Abee Shaybah/12639, Musnad Ahmad/7354, Musnad al-Bazzaar/8956, Saheeh Ibn Khuzaymah/2513, Saheeh Ibn Hibbaan/3696.

14 دَرْءُ الـمَفَاسِدِ أَوْلَى مِنْ جَلْبِ الـمَصَالِـح

edge and actions, and his character; [For such a man] it is legislated for him to perform the *hajj* every year.

Shaykh Muhammad ibn 'Uthaymeen

10. Performing Hajj if husband died and no Mahram exists

Question: Is it obligatory for a woman to perform *hajj* if she has lost her husband or if she does not have a *mahram* - but is [physically and financially] able [to perform *hajj*] and [that being] whilst she is in her *'iddah* after the death [of her husband]?[15]

Response: It is not obligatory upon a woman to perform *hajj* if she has no *mahram* who can travel with her to do so, and it is not permissible for her to leave [her home] to perform *hajj* whilst she is in her *'iddah* after the death [of her husband].

And with Allaah lies all success and may Allaah send prayers and salutations upon our Prophet (*sal-Allaahu 'alayhe wa sallam*) and his family and his Companions.

The Permanent Committee for Islaamic Research and Verdicts

11. Performing Hajj sooner or later

Question: Is the obligation of performing *hajj* to be undertaken promptly and without delay or [at one's leisure] whenever [one chooses to do

---

15 Fataawa al-Lajnah ad-Daa.imah lil-Buhooth al-'Ilmiyyah wal-Iftaa. - Volume 11, Page 94, Question 4 of Fatwa No.7316.

so]?[16]

Response: That which is correct is - it is obligatory to be carried out promptly and without delay, and it is not permissible for a person who is [physically and financially] able to perform *hajj* to the House of Allaah to delay it. And this is the case with all religious obligations - if they are not bound by time or reason[17], then their obligation is immediate.

Shaykh Muhammad ibn 'Uthaymeen

12. Performing Hajj with her grandsons

Question: Is it permissible for a woman to perform *hajj* without a *mahram*, with the knowledge that she has grandsons; So is it permissible for her to perform *hajj* with her grandsons? Please provide us a *fatwa*, and may Allaah reward you much with good.[18]

Response: It is not permissible for a woman to travel to perform *hajj* or other than that without her *mahram*; Bearing in mind that her grandchildren from both her sons and daughters are *mahram* for her, it is therefore permissible for her to perform *hajj* with [any of] them.

And with Allaah lies all success and may Allaah send prayers and salutations upon our Prophet (*sal-Allaahu 'alayhe wa sallam*) and his family and his Companions.

The Permanent Committee for Islaamic Research and Verdicts

---

16 Fataawa al-Hajj wal-'Umrah - Page 6.

17 Basis and cause.

18 Fataawa al-Lajnah ad-Daa.imah lil-Buhooth al-'Ilmiyyah wal-Iftaa. - Volume 11, Page 97, Fatwa No.7854.

13. Ruling regarding 'Umrah

Question: What is the ruling regarding *'umrah*?[19]

Response: As regards *'umrah*, then the scholars have differed in opinion regarding it's obligation; Some of them say it is obligatory, and some of them say it is recommended, and yet others amongst them differentiate between the residents of Makkah and other than them. So they say it is obligatory upon the non-residents of Makkah and not obligatory upon the residents of Makkah.

And I regard the preponderant opinion to be that it is obligatory upon every Muslim - residents of Makkah and other than them. However, it's obligation is lesser than the obligation of *hajj*. That is because the obligation of *hajj* is an asserted obligation since it is one of the pillars of Islaam, unlike *'umrah*.

Shaykh Muhammad ibn 'Uthaymeen

14. Maid performs Hajj with women or Hajj package group

Question: Is it permissible for me to send my maid for the obligatory *hajj* with a group of women travelling with a *hajj* package group[20]?[21]

Response: It is not permissible for a woman to travel for *hajj* or other than *hajj* except with a *mahram*, whether she is a maid or not, for that

---

19 Fataawa al-Hajj wal-'Umrah- Page 6-7.

20 Specialising in transporting and serving the hajj pilgrims for the duration of the hajj period.

21 al-Muntaqaa min Fataawa Ibn Fowzaan - Volume 3, Page 168, Fatwa No.252.

which the Prophet said (*sal-Allaahu 'alayhe wa sallam*) has said:

> **«It is not permissible for a woman who believes in Allaah and the Last Day to travel the distance of two days, except with a mahram»**[22]

And a group of women does not constitute a *mahram* and, likewise, nor does the *hajj* package group and this does not exclude her from that which is forbidden in the aforementioned *hadeeth*.

Shaykh Saalih ibn Fowzaan

15. Son performs Hajj from his father's wealth

Question: I have a son who is about 20 years [of age], and I have a car - but do not know how to drive; He (my son) is the one who drives, and I wanted to go for *hajj* in my car. On the basis that my son will perform his obligatory *hajj* and that he is [also] a student at school, my son heard that whoever has not done their obligatory *hajj*, then it is not permissible for them to do so from their father's wealth - even though I am financially comfortable; [Rather], he must [himself] work until he saves up enough [funds] for his *hajj*. Guide us, [and] may Allaah reward you?[23]

Response: If the son performs his obligatory *hajj* from his father's wealth, then his *hajj* is valid; And it is better for him to hasten in travelling for *hajj* with his father so he can assist him by driving the car, since this amounts to honouring his father.

---

22 Saheeh Muslim/420, Sunan at-Tirmidhee/1169, Musnad Ahmad/7222, Saheeh Ibn Khuzaymah/2523, Saheeh Ibn Hibbaan.

23 Fataawa al-Hajj wal-'Umrah waz-Ziyaarah - Page 18.

And with Allaah lies all success and may Allaah send prayers and salutations upon our Prophet (*sal-Allaahu 'alayhe wa sallam*) and his family and his Companions.

The Permanent Committee for Islaamic Research and Verdicts

16. The Hajj of one who does not pray

Question: What is the ruling concerning the one who performs *hajj* whilst he has abandoned prayer, either intentionally [because he believes he doesn't have to pray] or due to neglect? Is his *hajj* valid?[24]

Response: Whoever performs *hajj* whilst he does not pray because he believes it is not obligatory, then he has committed *kufr* by consensus [of the scholars] and his *hajj* is not valid. However, if he does not pray out of laziness and neglect, then in this [case] there is a difference of opinion amongst the people of knowledge. From amongst them are those who view his *hajj* as valid, and [likewise there are] those who view his *hajj* as invalid. And that which is correct is that it is invalid for that which the Prophet (*sal-Allaahu 'alayhe wa sallam*) said:

«The covenant that is between us and them (the disbelievers) is the prayer. Whoever abandons it has committed kufr»[25]

And He (*sal-Allaahu 'alayhe wa sallam*) also said:

---

24 Fataawa al-Hajj wal-'Umrah waz-Ziyaarah - Page 15.

25 Sunan at-Tirmidhee/2621, Sunan an-Nasaa.ee/463, Sunan Ibn Maajah/1079, Musannaf Ibn Abee Shaybah/30396, Musnad Ahmad/22937, Saheeh Ibn Hibbaan/1454, Sunan ad-Daaraqutnee/1751.

«Between a man and disbelief and polytheism is the abandoning of the prayer»[26]

And these [*ahaadeeth*] are general and encompass both - the one who believes it is not obligatory, and the one who does not pray out of laziness or neglect.

Shaykh 'Abdul-'Azeez ibn Baaz

17. The year in which the Hajj began

Question: What is the correct opinion concerning the *hijree* year in which the *hajj* [first] began (was legislated)?[27]

Response: The scholars have differed as to which year the *hajj* was legislated. So, it is said in the fifth year, and it is said in the sixth year, and it is said in the ninth year and it is [also] said in the tenth year. And the closest to that which is correct are the last two opinions and that it was either obligated in the ninth year or the tenth year.

And with Allaah lies all success and may Allaah send prayers and salutations upon our Prophet (*sal-Allaahu 'alayhe wa sallam*) and his family and his Companions.

The Permanent Committee for Islaamic Research and Verdicts

---

26 Musnad Ahmad/15183, al-Musnad al-Mustakhraj 'alaa Saheeh Muslim li-Abee Na'eem/245.

27 Fataawa al-Lajnah ad-Daa.imah lil-Buhooth al-'Ilmiyyah wal-Iftaa. - Volume 11, Page 10, Fatwa No.4624.

18. Wife performing 'Umrah with her father-in-law

Question: Is it permissible for my father to be a *mahram* for my wife to perform the *'umrah* whilst I remain in Riyadh?[28]

Response: The father-in-law is a *mahram* for his son's wife for the [purposes of the] *hajj* and other than that.

Shaykh 'Abdul-'Azeez ibn Baaz

Chapter Two

The ability to perform the Hajj

1. Came of Age during Hajj

Question: I performed the *hajj* with my family when I was young. On the 8th day of *Dhul-Hijjah* I had a wet dream and then took a ritual bath of purification, and then wore my *ihraam* and proceeded to [undertake the rites of] my *hajj*. After 7 years, I asked about my *hajj* - whether it was acceptable or not, and was informed that it was not. [This year] I wanted to perform *hajj* on behalf of my mother who died having only performed a single *hajj*, so will she be rewarded for this [forthcoming] *hajj* I intend to perform on her behalf, or am I required to perform the *hajj* for myself first, then her?[1]

Response: As soon as a young child comes of age during the *hajj* in 'Arafah or before it, and during the *'umrah* before the *tawaaf*, then this suffices his religious obligation. Since the questioner had a wet dream on the 8th day of *Dhul-Hijjah* and thereafter entered the state of *ihraam* and stood in 'Arafah, then his performance of the *hajj* fulfills his religious

---

1 Fataawa al-Hajj wal-'Umrah waz-Ziyaarah - Page 12.

obligation since he was in 'Arafah after coming of age. So he should consider that *hajj* for himself, and it is sufficient for him to now undertake
the *hajj* on behalf of his mother or other than her; Thereafter, maybe he
can repeat the *hajj* [voluntarily] for himself or his parents or whomso-
ever else he wishes.

Shaykh 'Abdullaah ibn Jibreen

2. Elderly woman performed Hajj without Mahram

Question: I performed *hajj* with a group of women [to whom I was
mahram], and an elderly lady who had no *mahram* [herself] joined
us - staying with the [group of] women. I undertook her expenses until
she completed the rites of *hajj* and returned home. Am I liable for any
sin for [doing] that?[2]

Response: Since this woman was elderly, and the questioner mentioned
there were other women [to whom he was *mahram*] with him and this
[elderly] woman joined [the group of women] because she did not have
anyone to accommodate her - and that she was unaware of [how to
complete] the rites of *hajj*, then [in this case] he has extended good
[towards her] in doing so.

And with Allaah lies all success and may Allaah send prayers and salutations upon our Prophet (*sal-Allaahu 'alayhe wa sallam*) and his family
and his Companions.

The Permanent Committee for Islaamic Research and Verdicts

---

2 Fataawa al-Hajj wal-'Umrah waz-Ziyaarah - Page 14-15.

3. Bank employee wishes to perform Hajj using his earnings

Question: I am an employee at a bank, so is it permissible for me to perform *hajj* from my earnings?[3]

Response: Working in a bank which deals with *ribaa* is not permissible.

This is because it is [considered] assisting in sin and evil. And also, the Prophet (*sal-Allaahu 'alayhe wa sallam*) cursed the one who benefited from *ribaa*, as well as the one responsible [for the transaction], the witnesses [to the transaction] and the one who writes [the transaction].

Therefore, the employee in reality is assisting the bank, even if he is just a [bank] clerk. So he is cursed according to the text of the *hadeeth*. Based upon this, the wage he earns is *haraam*, and it is not permissible for him to derive any benefit from it and nor to perform *hajj* with it. This is because the [performance of] *hajj* requires pure earnings from *halaal* [sources]. However, if he has [already] performed *hajj*, then his *hajj* is valid, but with sin [attached to it] (i.e. lesser in reward).

Shaykh Saalih ibn Fowzaan

4. Giving Zakaah to poor and destitute to perform Hajj

Question: If a poor and destitute person has not performed the obligatory *hajj* due to his financial inability to do so, in this case is it permissible to give him [funds] from the *zakaah* in order to facilitate his per-

---

3 al-Muntaqaa min Fataawa Fadheelatush-Shaykh Saalih ibn Fowzaan - Volume 4, Page121, Fatwa No.123.

forming the obligatory *hajj* himself?[4]

Response: There is no harm in giving the poor and destitute [funds] from the *zakaah* which will assist him in [performing] the *hajj*; And may Allaah grant everyone success.

Shaykh Saalih ibn Fowzaan

5. Performing Hajj with haraam money

Question: What is the ruling regarding someone who performed *hajj* with money which was *haraam*, i.e. from the profits of selling [illegal] drugs; [In addition to] sending tickets to his parents to perform *hajj*, with the knowledge that his money has been gathered from the sale of [illegal] drugs. Is such a *hajj* valid or not?[5]

Response: Performing *hajj* with money which is *haraam* does not affect the validity of the *hajj*; Instead, it incurs a sin and consequently a reduction in the reward for the *hajj* in accordance with the *haraam* funds used. So [using *haraam* funds] does not invalidate the *hajj*.

And with Allaah lies all success and may Allaah send prayers and salutations upon our Prophet (*sal-Allaahu 'alayhe wa sallam*) and his family and his Companions.

The Permanent Committee for Islaamic Research and Verdicts

---

4 ad-Durar an-Naadhirah fil-Fataawaa al-Mu'aasirah - Page 440.

5 Fataawaa al-Lajnah ad-Daa.imah lil-Buhooth al-'Ilmiyyah wal-Iftaa. - Volume 11, Page 43, Fatwa No.13619.

6. Performing Hajj whilst having outstanding loan to pay

Question: A Muslim wanted to perform the obligatory *hajj* whilst having an [outstanding] loan, so if he were to seek permission from the loaners and they permitted him to perform the *hajj*, would his *hajj* be acceptable?[6]

Response: If the situation is as you have mentioned, then there is no harm in performing the *hajj* before completing the payment [of the loan], as you have the permission of the loaners to perform *hajj* before completing payment [of the loan]. And in this situation, having borrowed [funds] does not affect [the validity of the *hajj*].

And with Allaah lies all success and may Allaah send prayers and salutations upon our Prophet (*sal-Allaahu 'alayhe wa sallam*) and his family and his Companions.

The Permanent Committee for Islaamic Research and Verdicts

7. The fear of being unable to complete the rites of Hajj

Question: If the pilgrim in the state of *ihraam* fears he will be unable to perform the rites [of *hajj* either] due to an illness or fear, then what should he do?[7]

Response: [This being the case, then] when the pilgrim assumes the state of *ihraam*, he should say:

---

6 Fataawa al-Lajnah ad-Daa.imah lil-Buhooth al-'Ilmiyyah wal-Iftaa. - Volume 11, Page 46, Fatwa No.5545.

7 Fataawa al-Hajj wal-'Umrah waz-Ziyaarah - Page 11.

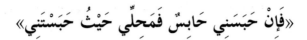

«فَإِنْ حَبَسَنِي حَابِسٌ فَمَحِلِّي حَيْثُ حَبَسْتَنِي»

«And if I am prevented by an obstacle, then indeed my place is where You prevent me»[8]

So if he fears anything may prevent him [from completing the rites of *hajj*] such as an illness, then it is from the *Sunnah* to pronounce this condition [at the time of assuming the *ihraam*] - as has been confirmed from the Prophet (*sal-Allaahu 'alayhe wa sallam*) that he commanded Dhibaa'ah bint az-Zubayr ibn 'Abdil-Muttalib with that when she complained to him [at the time of assuming the ihraam for *hajj*] that she was ill.

Shaykh 'Abdul-'Azeez ibn Baaz

8. The wording of the Condition

Question: Regarding the one who pronounces the condition[9] at the time of making the intention [in case he is unable to complete the *hajj* or the *'umrah*], is he required to pronounce it in the same wording as has been [authentically] reported from the Messenger of Allaah (*sal-Allaahu 'alayhe wa sallam*), or can he do so with any [appropriate] wording from himself?[10]

---

8 Saheeh al-Bukhaare/5089, Saheeh Muslim/154, Sunan Abee Daawood/1776, Sunan an-Nasaa.ee/2767, Sunan Ibn Maajah/2938, Musnad Ahmad/3117, Musnad al-Bazzaar/4731, Saheeh Ibn Hibbaan/3773, Sunan ad-Daaraqutnee/2429, Saheeh Ibn Hibbaan/3773.

9 «فَإِنْ حَبَسَنِي حَابِسٌ فَمَحِلِّي حَيْثُ حَبَسْتَنِي»

10 Fataawaa al-Hajj wal-'Umrah - Page 37.

<u>Response</u>: He is not required to use the same wording as has been [authentically] reported; That is because this wording [is only a condition and] is not something by which worship is sought, and [therefore] any wording by which worship is not sought - it's meaning [using appropriate wording] suffices.

Shaykh Muhammad ibn 'Uthaymeen

Chapter Three

The Ihraam and the Talbiyah

1. Applying perfume on ihraam before making intention

<u>Question</u>: What is the ruling regarding applying perfume on the *ihraam* before making the intention and uttering the *talbiyah*?[1]

<u>Response</u>: It is not befitting to apply perfume on the *ihraam*, rather, the *Sunnah* is to apply the perfume on the body such as the head, the beard and the armpits, and other such places. As for the *ihraam*, then do not apply perfume on them for that which the Prophet (*sal-Allaahu 'alayhe wa sallam*) said:

> «*Do not wear clothing which has been 'touched' by az-za'faraan or al-wars*»[2]

---

1 Majmoo' Fataawa Samaahatu ash-Shaykh 'Abdul-'Azeez ibn Baaz - Volume 6, Page 96, Fatwa No.46.

2 Saheeh al-Bukhaaree/1543, Saheeh Muslim/1177, Sunan an-Nasaa.ee/2675, Sunan Ibn Maajah/2929, Sunan ad-Daarimee/1839, Saheeh Ibn Khuzaymah/2597, Saheeh Ibn Hibbaan/3784.

So, the *Sunnah* is to apply perfume on the body only and as for the *ihraam*, then perfume is not to be applied on it. And if it has been, then it is not to be worn until it is washed or changed [for an unperfumed one].

Shaykh 'Abdul-'Azeez ibn Baaz

2. Changing or washing the ihraam

Question: Is it permissible to change the *ihraam* [in order] to wash it?[3]

Response: There is no harm in washing the *ihraam* [clothing] or changing it and using a new or washed *ihraam*.

Shaykh 'Abdul-'Azeez ibn Baaz

3. Covering the head whilst in the state of ihraam

Question: During the last *hajj*, I wore a skullcap whilst I was in the state of *ihraam*; I was unaware [of it's prohibition], so am I required to make an expiation? If so - and I do not have enough money for it - what should I do, may Allaah reward you with good?[4]

Response: In the name of Allaah, and all praise is due to Allaah [alone]... if you were ignorant [of the prohibition] and wore a headscarf or a skullcap on your head, or you had forgotten, then there is nothing (expia-

---

3 Fataawa al-Hajj wal-'Umrah waz-Ziyaarah - Page 53;
   Majmoo' Fataawa Samaahatu ash-Shaykh 'Abdul-'Azeez ibn Baaz - Volume 6, Page 96, Fatwa No.45.

4 ad-Durrar an-Naadhirah fil-Fataawa al-Mu'aasirah - Page 400;
   ad-Da'wah 1496 - Muharram 1416 AH.

tion) required of you, and all praise is due to Allaah [alone].

Shaykh 'Abdul-'Azeez ibn Baaz

4. Cut some hair before assuming state of ihraam

Question: Before assuming the state of *ihraam*, my wife cut some of her hair whilst in the bathroom, and then put her clothes on. Is there now anything required of her?[5]

Response: There is no harm in this nor any *fidyah* (expiation). This is because the prohibition of cutting the hair is after one has made the intention and assumed the state of *ihraam*. In this case, she had not yet made her intention and assumed the state of *ihraam*, nor had she put her clothes on. Therefore, there is no harm in this. Even if, [however], she had done this out of ignorance or forgetfulness once having assumed the state of *ihraam*, there would be nothing required of her in such circumstances.

Shaykh 'Abdullaah ibn Jibreen

5. Performing salaah specific to assuming state of ihraam

Question: Is there a specific *salaah* (prayer) for [once you have assumed] the state of *ihraam*?[6]

Response: There is no specific *salaah* for [once you have assumed] the state of *ihraam*. However, if a person arrives at the *meeqaat* and the

---

5 Fataawa al-Hajj wal-'Umrah waz-Ziyaarah - Page 57.

6 I'laam al-Mu'aasireen bi-Fataawa Ibn 'Uthaymeen - Page 141.

time for an obligatory prayer is [fast] approaching, then it is better he delays assuming the state of *ihraam* until he performs the obligatory prayer and thereafter assumes the state of *ihraam*.

Shaykh Muhammad ibn 'Uthaymeen

6. Pilgrim is in Minaa on 8th day of Dhul-Hijjah

Question: What is the ruling about the one who was in Minaa before the day of *tarwiyyah*[7]? Does he go to Makkah and assume the *ihraam* [from there] or can he do so [where he is] in Minaa?[8]

Response: For the one who is in Minaa, it is legislated for him to assume the *ihraam* in Minaa and all Praise is due to Allaah [alone]. There is no need to go to Makkah, rather, at the appropriate time he should utter the *talbiyah* for the *hajj* where he is.

Shaykh 'Abdul-'Azeez ibn Baaz

7. Shaved armpits whilst in state of ihraam

Question: A man assumed the state of *ihraam* for *'umrah*. Later, he remembered it is obligatory to shave the armpits, so he began to shave them whilst in the state of *ihraam*. He then proceeded for the *'umrah*. We request you explain the ruling [for this] and may you be rewarded.[9]

---

7 The 8th day of Dhul-Hijjah.

8 Majmoo' Fataawa Samaahatu ash-Shaykh 'Abdul-'Azeez ibn Baaz - Volume 6, Page 96, Fatwa No.47.

9 Majmoo' Fataawa Samaahatu ash-Shaykh 'Abdul-'Azeez ibn Baaz - Volume 6, Page 96, Fatwa No.48.

Response: It is not an obligatory condition to shave the armpits or pluck [the hairs] in order to assume the state of *ihraam*. Rather, it is recommended to pluck the hairs or remove them with something clean before assuming the state of *ihraam*, just as it is recommended to trim the moustache and nails and shave the pubic hairs if required (i.e. if they have sufficiently grown and need to be trimmed or cut).

It is not imperative this be done upon assuming the state of *ihraam*, rather it is enough if he does so before assuming the state of *ihraam* at home or on the way.

And if he is unaware of the *Sharee'ah* ruling [regarding this], there is no penalty for him should he shave his armpits. Similarly, for the one who has assumed the state of *ihraam*, then forgetfully does any of that which we have mentioned - as Allaah (*Subhaanahu wa Ta'aala*) says:

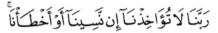

Our Lord, do not take us to account for that which we do forgetfully or mistakenly.[10]

...for that which has been confirmed from the Prophet (*sal-Allaahu 'alayhe wa sallam*), is that Allaah has responded to this supplication.

Shaykh 'Abdul-'Azeez ibn Baaz

8. Some hair fell out accidentally whilst in state of ihraam

Question: What should a woman who has assumed the state of *ihraam*

---

10 The Noble Qur.aan - Soorah al-Baqarah, Aayah 286.

do if a hair falls out without intention?[11]

Response: If some hair of either a male or female in the state of *ihraam* falls out when wiping the head during *wudhoo* or having a bath or shower, then this does not affect them (there is no harm). Likewise, if some hair falls from the beard or moustache of a man or anything from the nails, then none of this affects him - providing he did not intend so. Rather, that which is prohibited is if he intentionally cuts some of his hair or nails whilst he is in the state of *ihraam*, and likewise, the woman should not intend [any of] this. As regards that which falls unintentionally, then these are 'dead' hairs which fall when one moves or touches the head or hair. So, this does not affect the one who is in the state of *ihraam*.

And with Allaah lies all success and may Allaah send prayers and salutations upon our Prophet (*sal-Allaahu 'alayhe wa sallam*) and his family and his Companions.

The Permanent Committee for Islaamic Research and Verdicts

9. The ihraam of the small child

Question: If a small child is unable to do the *tawaaf* by himself, is it permissible to carry him and perform the *tawaaf*? And is the small child liable for any penalties if he misses any of the [prescribed] requirements of the *hajj*?[12]

Response: Since it is permissible for a small child to assume the state of *ihraam*, the guardian of the child then assumes complete responsibil-

---

11 Fataawa al-Hajj wal-'Umrah waz-Ziyaarah - Page 58.

12 Fataawa al-Hajj wal-'Umrah waz-Ziyaarah - Page 12.

ity for him. So he is required to clothe him as well as tie his *ihraam* and make the intention for the *hajj* on his behalf; [Likewise], utter the *talbiyah* on his behalf as well as holding his hand whilst performing the *tawaaf* and the *sa'ee*.

If, however, the child is unable, then there is no harm in carrying him; And in doing so, the correct opinion is for the guardian to perform the *tawaaf* [of seven circuits] only once - which will suffice both himself and the carried child.

[Whilst in the state of *ihraam*], if the small child were to do anything prohibited out of ignorance - such as wearing [stitched] clothing or covering his head, then he is not liable for any penalty since he did not intend this. If, however, he did so intentionally, such as in the case of wearing [stitched] clothing due to cold weather or the like, then his guardian is required to pay the penalty on his behalf.

Shaykh 'Abdullaah ibn Jibreen

10. The ihraam of the woman who wears socks and gloves

Question: What is the ruling regarding the *ihraam* of the woman who wears socks and gloves? Is it permissible for her to take off what she had put on when assuming the state of *ihraam*?[13]

Response: It is preferable that she wears socks or footwear - this is better for her, as well as covering herself sufficiently in loose clothing. There is no objection if she wears socks and then takes them off, just like a man who puts on shoes then takes them off when he wishes, there is no

---

13 Fataawa Muhimmah tata'allaq bil-Hajj wal-'Umrah - Page 18, Fatwa No.6.

problem in that. But it is not permissible for her to assume *ihraam* wearing gloves, because a woman is prohibited from wearing gloves whilst in the state of *ihraam*. She is also forbidden from wearing a veil over her face or any other thing similar to a veil, because the Messenger of Allaah (*sal-Allaahu 'alayhe wa sallam*) has forbidden this. But a woman is required to let her veil down over her face in the presence of non-*mahram* men. She is also required to do this during the *tawaaf* and *sa'ee*. 'Aa.ishah (*radhi-yAllaahu 'anhaa*) said:

'The riders had been passing by us while we were with the Messenger of Allaah (*sal-Allaahu 'alayhe wa sallam*). When they were opposite to us or parallel to us, we (the women) would let our veils down over our faces and heads, and when they passed away, we unveiled our faces'.[14]

According to the correct opinion, it is permissible for a man to wear slippers or shoes, even if they are not cut. On the other hand, most of the scholars are of the opinion that he should cut them. The correct opinion is that there is no obligation to cut them if he cannot manage [wearing] sandals. The Prophet (*sal-Allaahu 'alayhe wa sallam*) addressed the people of 'Arafah and said:

«He who is unable to manage the izaar, should wear trousers, and he who is unable to manage sandals should wear slippers»[15]

The Prophet (*sal-Allaahu 'alayhe wa sallam*) did not order for them to be cut. So, this indicates the revocation of the order of cutting them. And

---

14 Musannaf Ibn Abee Shaybah/14240, Musnad Ishaaq ibn Raahawayh/1189, al-Muntaqaa libnil-Jaarood/418.

15 Saheeh al-Bukhaaree/5853, Sunan ad-Daaraqutnee/2471.

Allaah is the Granter of all success.

Shaykh 'Abdul-'Azeez ibn Baaz

11. The time and place to assume the ihraam for Hajj

Question: If the pilgrim arrives in Makkah and performs 'umrah and [thereafter] relieves himself from the state of ihraam and remains in Makkah, when is he [then] required to assume the state of ihraam for the hajj, and from where?[16]

Response: At any time after sunrise, he is required to assume the state of ihraam for the hajj on the day of tarwiyyah[17], [that being] from the place where he is [currently] residing. He should then proceed to Minaa and perform there the Zhuhr, 'Asr, Maghrib [and] 'Ishaa [prayers] and [the following morning the] Fajr prayer.

Shaykh Muhammad ibn 'Uthaymeen

12. Two rak'ah prayer after assuming the state of ihraam

Question: Is the offering of a two rak'ah prayer a condition for assuming the state of ihraam or not?[18]

Response: That is not a condition, rather, the scholars have differed in opinion regarding its desirability. So the majority are of the opinion that the two rak'ah prayer is desirable; One would perform the ablution,

---

16 Fataawa al-Hajj wal-'Umrah - Page 45.

17 The 8th day of Dhul-Hijjah.

18 Fataawa al-Hajj wal-'Umrah waz-Ziyaarah - Page 48.

pray two *rak'ah*s then utter the *talbiyah*. And their reasoning for this is that the Messenger assumed the state of *ihraam* after the prayer, i.e. he performed the *Zhuhr* prayer, then assumed the state of *ihraam* on the farewell *hajj*, and He (*sal-Allaahu 'alayhe wa sallam*) said:

> *«Jibreel came to me from my Lord and told me to pray in this blessed valley...»*[19]

And this [*hadeeth*] suggests the legislation for the two *rak'ah* prayer, and this is the opinion of the majority of the people of knowledge.

And the others [from amongst the scholars] say:

This [*hadeeth*] does not suggest [the legislation for the two *rak'ah* prayer], rather the statement:

> *«Jibreel came to me from my Lord and told me to pray in this blessed valley...»*

...implies the intent is an obligatory prayer from the five [obligatory daily] prayers, and it is [therefore] not a provision for the two *rak'ah* prayer for the *ihraam*. So the fact that he assumed the *ihraam* after performing the obligatory prayer does not suggest the legislation for the two *rak'ah* prayer specific to the *ihraam*, rather, it suggests that it is better to assume the *ihraam* for *hajj* or *'umrah* after [offering] the [obligatory] prayer - if this is at all possible.

Shaykh 'Abdul-'Azeez ibn Baaz

---

19 Saheeh al-Bukhaaree/1534,2337and 7343, Sunan Abee Daawood/1800, Sunan Ibn Maajah/2976, Musnad Ahmad/161, Saheeh Ibn Khuzaymah/2617.

13. Verbally pronouncing the intention

<u>Question</u>: Regarding making the intention upon undertaking the rites [of *hajj* or *'umrah*], is it required to verbally pronounce it when uttering the *talbiyah*?[20]

<u>Response</u>: It is from the *talbiyah* to utter:

$$ \text{«لَبَّيْكَ عُمْرَةً»} $$

«Here I am [in response to Your call Allaah] performing *'umrah*»[21]

...if one is intending [to perform the] *'umrah*, and:

$$ \text{«لَبَّيْكَ حَجّاً»} $$

«Here I am [in response to Your call Allaah] performing *hajj*»[22]

...if one is intending [to perform the] *hajj*.

As for [making] the intention, then it is not permissible to verbally pronounce it; So, [for example] one must not say:

$$ \text{«اللّهُمَّ إِنِّي أُرِيْدُ عُمْرَةً»} $$

«Oh Allaah! I intend [to perform] *'umrah*»...

---

20 Fataawa al-Hajj wal-'Umrah - Page 18.

21 Saheeh Muslim/214, Sunan Abee Daawood/1795, Sunan an-Nasaa.ee/2729, Sunan Ibn Maajah/2968, Musnad Ahmad/11958, Saheeh Ibn Khuzaymah/2619, Saheeh Ibn Hibbaan/3930.

22 References as listed in footnote 21.

«أُرِيْدُ حَجّاً»

...or: «...I intend [to perform] *hajj*»;

...[uttering] this [or that which is similar] has not been [authentically] reported from the Prophet (*sal-Allaahu 'alayhe wa sallam*).

Shaykh Muhammad ibn 'Uthaymeen

14. Washing body to cool down whilst in state of ihraam

Question: Is it permissible for one who has assumed the state of *ihraam* to wash all his body with water so as to cool down, and why?[23]

Response: If it is hot, [then] it is permissible to wash all of the body so as to cool down, as this assists in activeness during worship. [However], care must be taken whilst washing, that no hair falls out.

And with Allaah lies all success and may Allaah send prayers and salutations upon our Prophet (*sal-Allaahu 'alayhe wa sallam*) and his family and his Companions.

The Permanent Committee for Islaamic Research and Verdicts

15. Wearing stitched belt and shoes in state of ihraam

Question: What is the ruling regarding wearing a stitched leather belt,

---

23 Fataawa al-Lajnah ad-Daa.imah lil-Buhooth al-'Ilmiyyah wal-Iftaa. - Volume 11, Page 184, Question 1 of Fatwa No.2173.

i.e. machine stitched, and likewise stitched shoes?[24]

Response: It is permissible for anyone who wishes to assume the state of *ihraam* for *hajj* or *'umrah* to wear a belt and shoes, even if they are both machine stitched.

And with Allaah lies all success and may Allaah send prayers and salutations upon our Prophet (*sal-Allaahu 'alayhe wa sallam*) and his family and his Companions.

The Permanent Committee for Islaamic Research and Verdicts

16. When to assume the ihraam for Hajj

Question: What is the [legislated] time [one is permitted] to assume the *ihraam* for *hajj*?[25]

Response: The [legislated] time [one is permitted] to assume the *ihraam* for *hajj* are the months which Allaah has mentioned in His statement:

$$ ٱلْحَجُّ أَشْهُرٌ مَّعْلُومَٰتٌ $$

The hajj is (in) the well-known months[26]

...and they are: *Shawwaal*, *Dhul-Qi'dah* and the [first] ten days of *Dhul-Hijjah*; So if he assumed the *ihraam* for *hajj* before these months, then according to the majority [of the people of knowledge] his [assuming

---

24 Fataawa al-Lajnah ad-Daa.imah lil-Buhooth al-'Ilmiyyah wal-Iftaa. - Volume 11, Page 170, Question 3 of Fatwa No.13366.

25 ad-Durar an-Naadhirah fil-Fataawa al-Mu'aasirah - Page 401.

26 The Noble Qur.aan - Soorah al-Baqarah, Aayah 197.

the state of] *ihraam* is invalid. And if he assumed the state of *ihraam* and stood in 'Arafah before the arrival of *Fajr* on the night of the tenth of *Dhul-Hijjah* then his *hajj* is valid. As for the *'umrah*, then he can assume the state of *ihraam* at anytime [without restriction].

Shaykh Saalih ibn Fowzaan

17. Whilst in ihraam, played with hair and some hair fell out

Question: He has a habit of playing with his hair when he is thinking; After he assumed the state of *ihraam*, he forgetfully did this and some hair fell out. Does he have to expiate [for his error]?[27]

Response: There is nothing required of him due to that which Allaah (*Subhaanahu wa Ta'aala*) mentions regarding the believers that they said:

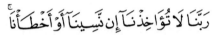

Our Lord! Punish us not if we forget or fall into error...[28]

...and Allaah has responded to their supplication as it has been mentioned on the authority of the Messenger of Allaah (*sal-Allaahu 'alayhe wa sallam*) that Allaah (*Subhaanahu wa Ta'aala*) said:

«I have done (this)».[29]

Shaykh 'Abdul-'Azeez ibn Baaz

---

27 Fataawa al-Hajj wal-'Umrah waz-Ziyaarah - Page 58.

28 The Noble Qur.aan - Soorah al-Baqarah, Aayah 286.

29 Saheeh Muslim/200.

Chapter Four

Performing Hajj on behalf of someone else

1. 16 year old dies without performing the Hajj

<u>Question</u>: My son died when he was 16 years old and had not performed the *hajj*. So, should I perform the *hajj* on his behalf?[1]

<u>Response</u>: If a boy or girl attains puberty or reaches 15 years of age, then it is obligatory upon him [or her] to perform the *hajj* if he [or she] is [physically and financially] able to do so. The performance of the *hajj* before attaining puberty does not suffice (i.e. it does not relieve him of the obligation of having to perform the obligatory *hajj*). So, if he died after coming of age and having had the ability, then perform the *hajj* on his behalf from his money or his guardian should perform the *hajj* on his behalf.

Shaykh 'Abdullaah ibn Jibreen

---

1 Fataawa al-Hajj wal-'Umrah waz-Ziyaarah - Page 25.

2. Did not set out for Hajj journey from father's hometown

Question: A man performed *hajj* this year on behalf of his deceased father. However, [when setting off for the *hajj* journey] he did not travel from his father's hometown; He is [now] asking regarding the validity of that *hajj* [on behalf of his father]?[2]

Response: It appears from the question of the inquirer that he undertook the *hajj* on behalf of his father at his own expense; So if the situation is as such, then there does not appear to be any problem with the validity of his *hajj* on his [father's] behalf - even if he did not set out for the *hajj* journey from his father's hometown.

And with Allaah lies all success and may Allaah send prayers and salutations upon our Prophet (*sal-Allaahu 'alayhe wa sallam*) and his family and his Companions.

The Permanent Committee for Islaamic Research and Verdicts

3. Performing tawaaf on behalf of the deceased

Question: Is it permissible for a person to perform *tawaaf* for his deceased parents or one of his relatives who has died?[3]

Response: There is no harm in someone performing the *hajj* or the *'umrah* on behalf of his parents or relatives. Likewise *inshaa.-Allaah*, there is no harm if he performed *tawaaf*, making the intention for its reward to [pass onto] one of his parents or relatives.

Shaykh 'Abdullaah ibn Jibreen

---

2 Fataawa al-Hajj wal-'Umrah waz-Ziyaarah - Page 145.

3 Fataawa al-Hajj wal-'Umrah waz-Ziyaarah - Page 87.

4. Voluntary Hajj on behalf of myself and my parents

Question: I am financially very comfortable, and all praise is due to Al-laah [alone]; Last year I paid three men to perform the [voluntary] *hajj* on behalf of myself, my father and my mother. Bearing in mind that I have already performed [my obligatory] *hajj*, I intend to continue to pay three men [every year] to perform the [voluntary] *hajj* on behalf of myself, my father and my mother, so long as I am alive. So, is there any religious prohibition in this?[4]

Response: May Allaah reward you with good. This [action of yours] is indicative of your keenness to do good. So long as you [yourself] have performed that which is obligatory upon you, and [now] you wish to do good for yourself and your parents then it would be better if you spent this money [allocated for the voluntary *hajj*s] on those who are needy from amongst the poor.

Shaykh Saalih ibn Fowzaan

5. Hajj on behalf of deceased mother, not deceased father

Question: After the death of my mother, I performed *hajj* on her behalf, and when my father died I did not perform *hajj* on his behalf. So, is there any sin upon me for not having performed *hajj* on his behalf?[5]

Response: There is no sin upon you for not having performed *hajj* on

---

4 al-Muntaqaa min Fataawa Shaykh Saalih al-Fowzaan - Volume 3, Page 184, Fatwa No.279.

5 Fataawa al-Lajnah ad-Daa.imah lil-Buhooth al-'Ilmiyyah wal-Iftaa. - Volume 11, Page 54, Fatwa No.1753.

behalf of your father. This is because it is not obligatory upon you to perform *hajj* on his behalf. However, from [the aspect of] honouring and being good [to your father] is to perform *hajj* on his behalf, as this is incorporated in the general statement of *ihsaan* which Allaah has commanded in His saying:

$$\text{وَبِٱلۡوَٰلِدَيۡنِ إِحۡسَٰنًا}$$

And be dutiful to your parents[6]

And with Allaah lies all success and may Allaah send prayers and salutations upon our Prophet (*sal-Allaahu 'alayhe wa sallam*) and his family and his Companions.

The Permanent Committee for Islaamic Research and Verdicts

6. Additional voluntary Hajj on behalf of my mother

Question: My mother performed the *hajj* seven times, so is it permissible for me myself to perform [yet another] *hajj* on her behalf?[7]

Response: Yes, it is permissible for you to perform [yet another] *hajj* on her behalf - an eighth *hajj* or more. This is [considered] from [extending] kindness [and honour] towards her, and therein is great reward for you if you have [already] performed the [obligatory] *hajj* for yourself.

Shaykh 'Abdul-'Azeez ibn Baaz

---

6 The Noble Qur.aan - Soorah al-Israa., Aayah 23.

7 Majmoo' Fataawa wa Rasaa.il 'Abdul-'Azeez ibn Baaz - Volume 16, Page 405.

7. Performing another 'Umrah having just done so already

Question: A man performed the 'umrah - and after completing it, went to Taif to do something. After completing what he had to do [in Taif] he wanted to perform 'umrah for a deceased [person], so is this permissible?[8]

Response: There is no harm in him doing this. If a person performs 'umrah, then leaves Makkah to go to Taif or Jeddah for [some] reason, [and whilst there] it occurs to him to do 'umrah for a deceased [person], then there is no harm in that, even if he repeated this [action] – there is no prohibition.

That which is forbidden is to remain in Makkah, and then depart to at-Tan'eem[9] so as to return to Makkah to do another 'umrah. This is what is forbidden.

Shaykh Muhammad ibn 'Uthaymeen

8. Hajj and charity on behalf of mother who did not pray

Question: Is it permissible for a daughter to perform hajj and give in charity on behalf of her deceased mother, knowing the mother did not pray during her life. What is the legal ruling regarding this [situation], bearing in mind that this daughter upholds and maintains that which is required of her from the pillars of Islaam?[10]

---

8 Liqaa.aat al-Baab al-Maftooh - Volume 1, Page 51, Number 86.

9 Popularly referred to as Masjid 'Aa.ishah.

10 Fataawa al-Lajnah ad-Daa.imah lil-Buhooth al-'Ilmiyyah wal-Iftaa. - Volume 11, Page 113, Question 2 of Fatwa No.6178.

Response: Whoever intentionally abandons praying because he does not think it is obligatory, then he has committed *kufr* according to the concensus of the scholars. And whoever abandons praying due to laziness and neglect, then he has [also] committed *kufr* according to the majority of the two opinions of the scholars, due to the saying of the Prophet (*sal-Allaahu 'alayhe wa sallam*):

«The covenant that is between us and them (the disbelievers) is the prayer. Whoever abandons it has committed kufr»[11]

...in addition to other evidences from the *Qur.aan* and the *Sunnah* in this matter.

So, based upon this, it is not permissible to perform *hajj*, nor to give in charity on behalf of anyone who has died and had abandoned the prayer, just as one cannot perform *hajj* nor give in charity on behalf of any of the *kuffaar*.

And with Allaah lies all success and may Allaah send prayers and salutations upon our Prophet (*sal-Allaahu 'alayhe wa sallam*) and his family and his Companions.

The Permanent Committee for Islaamic Research and Verdicts

9. Performing Hajj on behalf of a paralytic son

Question: I have a paralytic son, and am thinking about him performing

---

11 Sunan at-Tirmidhee/2621, Sunan an-Nasaa.ee/463, Sunan Ibn Maajah/1079, Musannaf Ibn Abee Shaybah/30396, Musnad Ahmad/22937, Saheeh Ibn Hibbaan/1454, Sunan ad-Daaraqutnee/1751.

hajj, because if he was to do the *hajj* himself, then I fear he will suffer harm. So, is it permissible for me to perform the *hajj* on his behalf?[12]

Response: If the son is [indeed] paralytic as you say, then it is permissible for you to perform the obligatory *hajj* on his behalf, if you have already performed [the obligatory] *hajj* for yourself.

Shaykh Muhammad ibn 'Uthaymeen

10. Performing Hajj on behalf of deceased grandparents

Question: My grandparents [both] from my father's side and my mother's side have died and I do not know whether they had fulfilled their obligation of performing *hajj* or not. So am I required to entrust someone to perform *hajj* on their behalf?[13]

Response: It is legislated for you to entrust those who are noble and trustworthy to perform *hajj* on behalf of every single one of them, so long as they (those you entrust) have [already] previously performed [the obligatory] *hajj* for themselves.

And with Allaah lies all success and may Allaah send prayers and salutations upon our Prophet (*sal-Allaahu 'alayhe wa sallam*) and his family and his Companions.

The Permanent Committee for Islaamic Research and Verdicts

---

12 Liqaa.aat al-Baab al-Maftooh - Volume 1, Page 45, Number 67.

13 Fataawa al-Lajnah ad-Daa.imah lil-Buhooth al-'Ilmiyyah wal-Iftaa. - Volume 11, Page 107, Question 12 of Fatwa No.6505.

11. Hajj or 'Umrah on behalf of parents who are alive

<u>Question</u>: Is it permissible for a Muslim to perform *hajj* or *'umrah* on behalf of his parents whilst they are still alive?[14]

<u>Response</u>: There is [some] explanation [required] in this issue:

As for the obligatory *hajj* and the obligatory *'umrah*, then it is not permissible to appoint anyone on their behalf, unless there is something permanent preventing them from performing *hajj* or *'umrah*, such as the one who is suffering from a prolonged illness as a result of which he is unable to travel for *hajj* to undertake the rites of *hajj*, or the one who is elderly [and] senile; This is based upon the hadeeth of the woman who said to the Prophet (*sal-Allaahu 'alayhe wa sallam*) that it has become incumbent upon her father to perform the obligatory *hajj*, however he is unable to travel, 'so should I perform *hajj* on his behalf?' The Prophet (*sal-Allaahu 'alayhe wa sallam*) said to her:

«Perform the hajj on behalf of your father»[15]

As for the voluntary *hajj*, then the issue is quite open; There is no harm in him performing *hajj* on behalf of his parents, even if they were able [to do so themselves], [and] this is the opinion of a group of scholars.

Shaykh Saalih ibn Fowzaan

---

14 al-Muntaqaa min Fataawa Shaykh Saalih al-Fowzaan - Volume 5, Page 160, Fatwa No.239.

15 Sunan at-Tirmidhee/930, Sunan an-Nasaa.ee/2637, Sunan Ibn Maajah/2904, Musannaf Ibn Abee Shaybah/15007, Musnad Ahmad/2189, Sunan ad-Daarimee/1879, Saheeh Ibn Khuzaymah/3035, Saheeh Ibn Hibbaan/3991, Sunan ad-Daaraqutnee/2710.

12. Performing 'Umrah on behalf of the deceased

Question: I made the intention to perform 'umrah for my eldest brother since he has passed away. So I want to know, is this act from the religious acts which (whose reward) will reach the deceased?[16]

Response: Yes, because this is something good, [that being] you performing 'umrah on behalf of your deceased brother whether it be the obligatory ['umrah] or the recommended [voluntary 'umrah] - so this is a great act; However, [the permissibility of this is] based upon the condition that you have already performed the obligatory 'umrah for yourself first, and Allaah has the Complete Knowledge of All affairs.

Shaykh Saalih ibn Fowzaan

13. Hajj on behalf of someone else for money

Question: Is it permissible for a person to perform the obligation of the hajj on behalf of someone else who is financially and physically able [to perform the hajj himself] in exchange for money?[17]

Response: Whoever is able to perform the obligation of hajj himself, then it is not permissible for him to appoint someone else to perform hajj on his behalf, and he will not be rewarded for it [by Allaah] if he does so.

---

16 al-Muntaqaa min Fataawa Shaykh Saalih al-Fowzaan - Volume 5, Page 160, Fatwa No.240.

17 al-Muntaqaa min Fataawa Shaykh Saalih al-Fowzaan - Volume 3, Page 190, Fatwa No.291.

As for the one who is unable to perform *hajj* himself due to a condition which permanently prevents him from doing so, then it is permissible for him to appoint someone else to perform *hajj* on his behalf.

And there is no harm in him taking money [for performing *hajj*] if he intends by it to use it for *hajj*, and not intending [to seek] any financial enjoyment (benefit) [by undertaking the performance of *hajj*]. And we have a rule some of the scholars use which has been extracted from the authentic evidences, that being:

'Whoever [makes the intention to] perform *hajj* to seek financial gain, then he should not perform *hajj*. And whoever takes money in order to perform *hajj*, then he should [go ahead and] perform *hajj*.'

And the meaning of this is, whoever uses money as a means to perform *hajj*, then there is no harm in that, and whoever uses the [performance of] *hajj* as a means to earn money then that is not permissible.

Shaykh Saalih ibn Fowzaan

14. That which benefits the deceased by way of the living

Question: What are the things which benefit the deceased by way of the living? And is there a difference between physical and non-physical acts of worship? We hope you will clarify these issues for us, and outline a principle which we could refer to whenever we come across issues such as these; [Please] provide us with a *fatwa*, and may Allaah bless you [in your affairs]?[18]

---

18 al-Muntaqaa min Fataawa Shaykh Saalih al-Fowzaan - Volume 2, Page 161, Fatwa No.139.

Response: The deceased benefits from the action[s] of the living by way of that which [authentic] evidence indicates [permissibility for] - from supplication [for the deceased], and the seeking of forgiveness for him (the deceased) and giving in charity on his (the deceased's) behalf and [performing] *hajj* and *'umrah* on his behalf and paying off his debts and executing his Islaamic will; All of these have been legislated for.

And some of the scholars have attached to this all acts of worship which a Muslim does intending their reward for a[nother] Muslim who is alive or dead. However, that which is correct is to limit [oneself] to that which [authentic] evidence indicates [permissibility for] as this will be in accordance with His (*Subhaanahu wa Ta'aala*) saying:

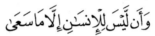

And that man can have nothing but what he does (good or bad)[19]

...and Allaah has the Complete Knowledge of All affairs.

Shaykh Saalih ibn Fowzaan

15. The Hajj of the disabled

Question: Is *hajj* obligatory upon the disabled (incapacitated) or not?[20]

Response: Whoever is able to perform *hajj* with his money, but is unable to physically undertake the *hajj* due to a persistent [physically] prohibiting factor, then he is required to appoint someone to perform the

---

19 The Noble Qur.aan - Soorah an-Najm, Aayah 39.

20 ad-Durar an-Naadhirah fil-Fataawa al-Mu'aasirah - Page 434.

obligatory *hajj* on his behalf - with the condition that the appointee has already performed [the obligatory] *hajj* for himself.

Shaykh Saalih ibn Fowzaan

16. Forgot to pronounce intention on behalf of mother

Question: What is the ruling concerning the one who performed *hajj* on behalf of his mother and at the *meeqaat* he uttered the *talbiyah* for the *hajj* and did not do so for his mother?[21]

Response: As long as his intention was for *hajj* on behalf of his mother, even if he forgot, the *hajj* is [acceptable] for his mother since the intention is a stronger [argument], for that which the Prophet (*sal-Allaahu 'alayhe wa sallam*) said:

«*Actions are but by intention*»[22]

So, if the intention in his coming was to perform *hajj* on behalf of his mother or father, and then he forgot [to make the intention] when he assumed the state of *ihraam*, the *hajj* is [acceptable] for whomever he had intended it for, either his mother, father or other than them.

Shaykh 'Abdul-'Azeez ibn Baaz

---

21 Majmoo' Fataawa Samahatu ash-Shaykh 'Abdul-'Azeez ibn Baaz - Volume 6, Page 116, Fatwa No.74.

22 Saheeh al-Bukhaaree/1, Sunan Abee Daawood/2201, Sunan Ibn Maajah/4227.

Question: A man made the intention to perform *hajj* for himself, since he had already previously performed *hajj*. He then decided to change his intention for his relative whilst in 'Arafah. So what is the ruling regarding this, and is it permissible?[23]

Response: When a person assumes the state of *ihraam* for *hajj* for himself, he cannot thereafter change the intention, neither en route, nor in 'Arafah, nor any other place. Rather, he is required to complete the *hajj* for himself and not to change [the intention] for his father, nor his mother, and nor anyone else.

The *hajj* is [now] specific for him because of the saying of Allaah (*Subhaanahu wa Ta'ala*):

$$\text{وَأَتِمُّوا۟ ٱلْحَجَّ وَٱلْعُمْرَةَ لِلَّهِ}$$

...and complete Hajj and 'Umrah for (the Sake of) Allaah[24]

So, if he assumes the state of *ihraam* for himself, it is obligatory he [continues and] completes it for himself. [Likewise], if he assumes the state of *ihraam* for someone else, it is obligatory he [continues and] completes it for someone else, and does not change [the intention] once he has assumed the state of *ihraam*.

And with Allaah lies all success and may Allaah send prayers and salutations upon our Prophet (*sal-Allaahu 'alayhe wa sallam*) and his family

---

23 Fataawa al-Hajj wal-'Umrah waz-Ziyaarah - Page 27.

24 The Noble Qur.aan - Soorah al-Baqarah, Aayah 196

and his Companions.

The Permanent Committee for Islaamic Research and Verdicts

Chapter Five

The Mawaaqeet

1. Travelled from Madeenah and assumed ihraam in Jeddah

Question: I am a student in Madeenah; I wanted to perform '*umrah* but was unable to find a car to take me directly to Makkah. Instead, I travelled to Jeddah first, where I assumed the state of *ihraam*. So, am I liable for any penalty? And was it correct for me to have assumed the state of *ihraam* in Jeddah?[1]

Response: If the situation is as you have mentioned, that you wanted to perform '*umrah*, and you travelled from Madeenah to Jeddah and assumed the state of *ihraam* in Jeddah, then you have erred. This is because you passed the *meeqaat* of the people of Madeenah [thereby entering the *meeqaat* zone] without assuming the state of *ihraam*. So you must seek forgiveness from Allaah and never repeat this act again.

As a result of passing the *meeqaat* without assuming the state of *ihraam*, you are required at any time to sacrifice one goat [of a quality which

---

1 Fataawa al-Hajj wal-'Umrah waz-Ziyaarah - Page 36.

satisfies the conditions for the *udh.hiyyah* sacrifice] in Makkah and distribute [the meat] to the poor and needy there, without eating any of it
yourself.

And with Allaah lies all success and may Allaah send prayers and salutations upon our Prophet (*sal-Allaahu 'alayhe wa sallam*) and his family
and his Companions.

The Permanent Committee for Islaamic Research and Verdicts

2. Assuming ihraam in Jeddah after arriving by air

Question: Some of them issue legal rulings for those pilgrims arriving
by air to assume their *ihraam* from Jeddah, whilst others disapprove of
that. So, what is the correct opinion regarding this issue?[2]

Response: It is obligatory upon all the pilgrims arriving by air, sea and
land to assume their *ihraam* at the [nearest] *meeqaat* they intend
to pass through - whether by land, air or sea; This is based upon the
statement of the Prophet (*sal-Allaahu 'alayhe wa sallam*) when the
meeqaat's were designated:

*«They are for them (their residents) and whoever
comes to them who is not of their people intending
[to perform] the hajj and the 'umrah»*[3]

Shaykh 'Abdul-'Azeez ibn Baaz

---

2 Fataawa al-Hajj wal-'Umrah waz-Ziyaarah - Page 34.

3 Saheeh al-Bukhaaree/1524, al-Musnad al-Mustakhraj 'alaa Saheeh Muslim li-Abee
Na'eem/2698.

3. Assuming the ihraam from Madeenah

Question: There are some pilgrims who arrive from their countries intending [to travel first to] Madeenah; So they pass the *meeqaat* [which was more appropriate for them upon entry into Saudi Arabia]. Are they required to assume the state of *ihraam* from their *meeqaat*, and then proceed to Madeenah in *ihraam*, or should they travel to Madeenah without assuming the state of *ihraam*, and then when they depart to Makkah they assume the state of *ihraam* from the *meeqaat* of the people of Madeenah[4]?[5]

Response: They should travel to Madeenah without assuming the state of *ihraam*. That is because they do not intend [to travel first to] Makkah, rather they intend [to travel first to] Madeenah, and then [from there] travel [to Makkah]. So when they depart from Madeenah, it is then that they intend [to travel to] Makkah; So they must assume the state of *ihraam* fom the *meeqaat* of the people of Madeenah which is 'Dhul-Hulayfah', and which is now called 'Abyaar 'Alee'.

Shaykh Muhammad ibn 'Uthaymeen

4. Assuming state of ihraam whilst travelling in an airplane

Question: When should one, intending *hajj* or *'umrah* - and travelling by air, assume the state of *ihraam*?[6]

Response: The traveller either by air or sea should assume the state of

---

4 Dhul-Hulayfah / Abyaar 'Alee.

5 Fataawa al-Hajj wal-'Umrah - Page 17.

6 Fataawa al-Hajj wal-'Umrah waz-Ziyaarah - Page 32.

ihraam when the *meeqaat* is approaching. For example, the traveller, when apporaching the *meeqaat* either from air or the sea, should assume the state of *ihraam* just before [they approach the *meeqaat*] by a little, out of precaution for the speed of the airplane, ship or steamer.

Shaykh 'Abdullaah ibn Jibreen

5. Jeddah is within the Meeqaat Zone

Question: What is the ruling regarding the pilgrim who made the intention for *hajj*, arrived by air and landed in Jeddah without having assumed the state of *ihraam*; He then assumed the state of *ihraam* in Jeddah. So, is he liable for any penalty?[7]

Response: If the airplane lands in Jeddah and he is travelling from ash-Shaam[8] or Egypt[9], then he is required to assume the state of *ihraam* at Raabigh. So he travels to Raabigh by car or any other available mode of transport, and he then assumes the state of *ihraam* from Raabigh and not from Jeddah.

And likewise for those arriving from Najd[10], and have not assumed the state of *ihraam* until they arrive at Jeddah; They are then required to travel to as-Sayl which is Waadi Qarn and assume the state of *ihraam* from there. So if he assumed the state of *ihraam* from Jeddah and does not travel to [the appropriate *meeqaat* to assume the state of *ihraam*

---

7 Fataawa al-Hajj wal-'Umrah waz-Ziyaarah - Pages 34-35.

8 To the North of Saudi Arabia - Palestine, Syria and Jordan.

9 To the West of Saudi Arabia.

10 To the East of Saudi Arabia.

from there], then he is required to pay a compulsory penalty consisting of sacrificing [either] one sheep [of a quality which satisfies the conditions for the *udh.hiyyah* sacrifice] in Makkah for the poor and needy there, or a seventh part of a camel or a seventh part of a cow for his *hajj* or *'umrah*.

Shaykh 'Abdul-'Azeez ibn Baaz

6. When to assume state of ihraam in an airplane

Question: A man wanted to perform *hajj* or *'umrah*, and assumed the state of *ihraam* on the airplane. He does not know the location of the *meeqaat*, so should he delay assuming the state of *ihraam* once he reaches Jeddah or not?[11]

Response: If he intended *hajj* or *'umrah* [whilst arriving] by air, then he should have a bath at home and wear the *izaar* and *ridaa* (*ihraam* clothing), if he wishes. So, if there is only a little time before approaching the *meeqaat*, he should assume the state of *ihraam* according to what he intends - whether for *hajj* or *'umrah*, so there is no hardship in this. And if he does not know about the *meeqaat*, then he should ask the pilot of the airplane, one of the hostesses or one of the passengers whom he trusts and who has some experience in this.

And with Allaah lies all success and may Allaah send prayers and salutations upon our Prophet (*sal-Allaahu 'alayhe wa sallam*) and his family and his Companions.

The Permanent Committee for Islaamic Research and Verdicts

---

11 Fataawa al-Hajj wal-'Umrah waz-Ziyaarah - Page 34.
    Fataawa al-Lajnah ad-Daa.imah lil-Buhooth al-'Ilmiyyah wal-Iftaa. - Volume 11, Page 53, Question 3 of Fatwa No.1693

Chapter Six

Things to beware of upon assuming the state of Ihraam

1. Had wet dream whilst asleep in Minaa

Question: Whilst I was performing the obligatory *hajj*, one night, while I was in Minaa, I had a wet dream and was unable to take a *ghusl*. So, am I eligible for any penalty?[1]

Response: Having a wet dream whilst in the state of *ihraam* for the *hajj* or the *'umrah* does not affect the validity of the *hajj* nor the *'umrah*. Whoever experiences this should take a *ghusl* for the *janaabah* after waking up from the sleep - if he saw semen; He is not eligible for any penalty because he did not choose to have a wet dream.

And with Allaah lies all success and may Allaah send prayers and salutations upon our Prophet (*sal-Allaahu 'alayhe wa sallam*) and his family and his Companions.

The Permanent Committee for Islaamic Research and Verdicts

---

1 Fataawa al-Hajj wal-'Umrah waz-Ziyaarah - Page 64.

2. Placing something on head during state of ihraam

Question: You have [previously] mentioned, whilst in the state of *ihraam*, it is not allowed to cover the head, nor place anything on the head which touches it - such as a headscarf or skullcap; So, does this also include placing a piece of paper, cardboard or blanket on the head?[2]

Response: Yes, it includes [all of] these. Therefore, should he need to shade his head, he can raise it[3] above his head a little so it does not touch it.

Shaykh Muhammad ibn 'Uthaymeen

3. Things to beware of whilst in the state of ihraam

Question: What are the things that the *muhrim* needs to be aware of?[4]

Response: The *muhrim* must be aware of nine things which the scholars have mentioned, and these are:

1. Cutting / trimming [any] hair;
2. Cutting / trimming the nails;
3. Applying perfume;
4. Wearing [any] stitched garment;
5. Covering the head;

---

2 Fataawa al-Hajj wal-'Umrah - Page 40-41.

3 The shade, i.e. headscarf, piece of paper, cardboard, blanket or anything else used for shading the head.

4 Majmoo' Fataawa Samahatu ash-Shaykh 'Abdul-'Azeez ibn Baaz - Volume 6, Page 97, Fatwa No.49.

6. Hunting game;

7. Sexual intercourse;

8. Entering into a contract of marriage;

9. Touching one's wife sexually.

All of these are impermissible for the *muḥrim* until he relieves himself from the first state of *iḥraam* [during the *ḥajj*], whereby all of the afore-mentioned are permissible, except sexual intercourse. So, when he relieves himself from the second state of *iḥraam*, sexual intercourse is then also permissible.

Shaykh 'Abdul-'Azeez ibn Baaz

4. Wiped face after supplicating and two eyelashes fell off

<u>Question</u>: I performed the obligatory *ḥajj* 2 years ago, and that was the first time. On the day of 'Arafah, as I was supplicating to my Lord on that great day my eyes reddened and when I finished, I wiped my hands over my face[5] and tears, as a result of which two eyelashes fell off. I had not intended this, so am I liable for any penalty in this case?[6]

<u>Response</u>: May Allaah accept from you and us and may He multiply your reward for your adherence and your concentration and your deed which you had intended for the Face (Sake) of Allaah. As for that which you have mentioned of your eyelashes falling off, then you are not liable for any penalty, *inshaa.-Allaah*, since you had not intended that, and it was not done intentionally. Allaah has forgiven that which is done mistakenly

---

5 Wiping the face after supplicating is not from the Sunnah, rather it is an innovation, and this fatwa does not in any way or form imply it's permissibility or acceptance.

6 Fataawa al-Hajj wal-'Umrah waz-Ziyaarah - Page 58.

or forgetfully, and may Allaah grant you success.

Shaykh 'Abdullaah ibn Jibreen

5. Went to sleep covering my head whilst in state of ihraam

<u>Question</u>: After having assumed the state of *ihraam* at Abyaar 'Alee [7], we proceeded on our journey to Makkah, [whereupon] I was struck with severe fever. So I slept and covered my head. Am I now liable for any penalty? [8]

<u>Response</u>: It is obligatory upon you to pay a *fidyah*, which consists of fasting three [consecutive] days, or feeding six needy people, or sacrificing a sheep in the *Haram* (Makkah) sanctuary.

And with Allaah lies all success and may Allaah send prayers and salutations upon our Prophet (*sal-Allaahu 'alayhe wa sallam*) and his family and his Companions.

The Permanent Committee for Islaamic Research and Verdicts

6. Wore a pair of shorts whilst in the state of ihraam

<u>Question</u>: A year ago, I performed *'umrah* and was ignorant of some of the conditions. When I assumed the state of *ihraam* at the *meeqaat*, I wore a pair of shorts and was ignorant about this matter. When I returned, some people informed me that this is not permissible, so I per-

---

7 Dhul-Hulayfah, Madeenah.

8 Fataawa al-Lajnah ad-Daa.imah lil-Buhooth al-'Ilmiyyah wal-Iftaa. - Volume 11, Page 182, Question 2 of Fatwa No.9555.

formed 'umrah [again] this year. Am I still liable for any penalty in this case [when I wore a pair of shorts last year]?[9]

Response: You are not liable for any penalty, since you were ignorant of the ruling. So, ignorance is an excuse in this impermissible act, whilst the expiation (penalty) is [only] required from one who knows of the ruling and [then] did so intentionally. So you are not required to repeat the 'umrah since you have not done anything to spoil it, and the second 'umrah is considered a supererogatory one.

Shaykh 'Abdullaah ibn Jibreen

6

---

9   Fataawa al-Hajj wal-'Umrah waz-Ziyaarah - Page 59-60.

Chapter Seven

Menses and post partum bleeding

1. Assumed ihraam whilst on her menses

Question: Whilst on her menses, a woman assumed the state of *ihraam* for *hajj* from as-Sayl[1]. Upon arriving in Makkah she travelled to Jeddah for a necessity, and whilst in Jeddah she completed her menses and took a ritual bath of purification and then brushed her hair and then [proceeded to Makkah where] she completed [the rituals of] her *hajj*. So is her *hajj* valid, and is she liable for any penalty?[2]

Response: There is no harm in that, and her journey to Jeddah whilst she was on her menses does not affect [the validity of] her *hajj*, and [as such] she is not liable for any penalty; Likewise, [is the case] with brushing her hair - so long as this did not involve any perfume or cutting of the hair.

---

1 Meeqaat for the pilgrims arriving from Najd. It is also known as Waadi Qarn and Qarn al-Manaazil.

2 Fataawa al-Hajj wal-'Umrah waz-Ziyaarah - Page 67.

If she did use perfume or cut any of her hair, then she is not liable to any penalty if she was forgetful or ignorant [of the ruling]. If, however, she intentionally did so and was aware of the legal ruling, then she is required to make an expiation for using perfume as well as for cutting her hair; The expiation - each for cutting [the hair] and [using] perfume - will be [in the form of] feeding six poor and needy people half a *saa'* from the food of the land or sacrificing a sheep or fasting three days.

Shaykh 'Abdul-'Azeez ibn Baaz

2. Menses started before performing Tawaaf al-Ifaadhah

Question: If a woman started her menses before performing *tawaaf al-ifaadhah*, then should she travel to her home [remaining there until she completes her menses and purifies herself and] then return to perform *tawaaf al-ifaadhah* or should she wait [in Makkah] until she [completes her menses and] purifies herself and then perform *tawaaf* [al-ifaadhah]?[3]

Response: If a woman started her menses before *tawaaf al-ifaadhah*, then her *mahram* should wait with her until she [completes her menses and] purifies herself [and thereafter perform *tawaaf al-ifaadhah*]. If she is unable to do that, then she should travel [to her home, remaining there] until she [completes her menses and] purifies herself, and thereafter she should return to complete [the rites of] her *hajj*; [Importantly], throughout this time, her husband is not to engage [in sexual relations] with her.

[However], if she [was to travel home and thereafter] is unable to re-

---

3 I'laam al-Mu'aasireen bi-Fataawa Ibn 'Uthaymeen - Page 146-147.

turn [to Makkah to complete the rites of her *hajj*] because she lives in another country [for example], then she is required to suitably cover her vaginal area and perform *tawaaf* due to necessity.

Shaykh Muhammad ibn 'Uthaymeen

3. Taking pills to prevent menses during Hajj or 'Umrah

Question: Is it permissible for a woman to take [pills/medication] to prevent [the onset of] her menses so she can perform the rites of *hajj* or *'umrah* with ease?[4]

Response: I do not see any harm in [a woman] taking this medical treatment, with the condition that the doctor [in his/her professional opinion] does not see any harm in the woman taking these pills. So, the [basic] principle in these matters is permissibility, and [so long as] there is no falling into sin in this act.

Shaykh Muhammad Naasiruddeen al-Albaanee

4. Taking pills to prevent onset of menses

Question: What is the ruling regarding a woman using pills to prevent the onset of her menses during the days of *hajj*?[5]

Response: There is no harm in that since therein is an advantage and benefit that will allow her to perform *tawaaf* with the [other] pilgrims, and also that she does not delay anyone who accompanied her.

Shaykh 'Abdul-'Azeez ibn Baaz

---

4 Fataawa Muhimmah li-Nisaa. al-Ummah - Page 53.

5 Fataawa al-Hajj wal-'Umrah waz-Ziyaarah - Page 15.

5. Woman on her menses wishes to sit in the Mas'aa

Question: Is it permissible for a woman on her menses to sit in the *mas'aa*?[6]

Response: Yes, it is permissible for the woman on her menses to sit in the *mas'aa*, because the *mas'aa* is not considered [part of] *al-Masjid al-Haraam*. In that case, if the woman's menses started after the *tawaaf* and before the *sa'ee*, then she [is permitted] to do *sa'ee* because the *sa'ee* is not the *tawaaf*. Also, it is not a requirement [to be in the state of] purity. So, based upon this, we say that if the woman on her menses was to sit in the *mas'aa* waiting for her husband (family), then there is no harm in her doing this.

Shaykh Muhammad ibn 'Uthaymeen

---

6 Fataawa al-Hajj wal-'Umrah waz-Ziyaarah - Page 69.

Chapter Eight

The Tawaaf and the Sa'ee

1. Began Sa'ee at Marwah and finished at Safaa

Question: I am an old man. I did *tawaaf* for *'umrah* and then the seven laps for *sa'ee*. However, I began [the *sa'ee*] at *Marwah* and ended at *Safaa* and upon completing the *'umrah*, I got dressed into normal clothing.[1]

Response: You are required to do one more lap since you have missed one. However, if you had completed eight laps, there is no harm - since the first lap is regarded as extra and therefore does not affect [the validity of your *sa'ee*].

What is understood then is that if he began at *Marwah* and ended at *Safaa* after eight laps, then from that will be seven complete laps. However, if there were just seven laps then he has missed one, and he is required to do one more lap in order to complete that which is required of him. After doing this, he must either cut or shave his hair so as to complete

---

1 Fataawa al-Hajj wal-'Umrah waz-Ziyaarah - Page 92.

the 'umrah. The previous cutting of the hair is not sufficient because he did so prior to [correctly] completing the sa'ee, since the first lap with which he began at Marwah is not considered.

Shaykh 'Abdul-'Azeez ibn Baaz

2. Bribing the policeman to kiss al-Hajar al-Aswad

Question: [Whilst on hajj] a man with his mother approached al-Hajar al-Aswad[2] to kiss it, but were unable to do so due to the crowds. So, he gave the policeman [standing] by al-Hajar al-Aswad ten riyals[3]. He (the policeman) then distanced the people from al-Hajar al-Aswad to allow this man and his mother to kiss it. Is this permissible or not? And is his hajj valid or not?[4]

Response: If the matter is as mentioned, then the amount this man paid to the policeman is [considered as] bribery and not permissible for him to have paid. [Importantly], the kissing of al-Hajar al-Aswad is a Sunnah, and neither is it from the pillars of hajj nor from its requirements. So, whoever is able to touch or kiss it, without harming anyone, then it is permissible for him. And if he is unable to touch or kiss it, then he should touch it with a stick and then kiss it (the stick). And if he is unable to touch it with his hand or the stick, then he should make a sign towards it as he comes into line with it (opposite) and should say: 'Allaahu Akbar'. This is the Sunnah. As for giving the bribe, then that is not permissible; Not for the one performing tawaaf and nor for the

---

2 The Black Stone; located on the corner of the Ka'bah, at the starting point of the tawaaf.

3 Approximately £1.80/$2.20 at current rates.

4 Fataawa al-Hajj wal-'Umrah waz-Ziyaarah - Pages 88-89.

policeman. They are both required to repent to Allaah for that.

And with Allaah lies all success and may Allaah send prayers and salutations upon our Prophet (*sal-Allaahu 'alayhe wa sallam*) and his family and his Companions.

The Permanent Committee for Islaamic Research and Verdicts

3. Clinging on to the Kiswah of the Ka'bah

Question: What is the ruling regarding those who cling onto the *Kiswah* of the *Ka'bah* and engage in prolonged supplications?[5]

Response: There is no evidence from the *Sunnah* [to support] the action of these people, rather it is an innovation; It is befitting the students of knowledge explain this to them, that it is not from the practice of the Prophet (*sal-Allaahu 'alayhe wa sallam*).

As for clinging on to the *Ka'bah* by standing between *al-Hajar al-Aswad* and the door, then this act has been [authentically] reported from the Companions [of the Prophet (*sal-Allaahu 'alayhe wa sallam*)], so there is no harm in in doing so. As [for what] we see nowadays, when it is busy and congested, it is not befitting to engage in anything which causes harm and injury to others - [particularly] by doing that which is not [even] an obligatory act.

Shaykh Muhammad ibn 'Uthaymeen

---

5 Fataawa al-Hajj wal-'Umrah - Page 58.

4. Completing the Tawaaf with the Takbeer

Question: Is the performance of the *tawaaf* completed with the *takbeer* at *al-Hajar al-Aswad* just as at the beginning [of the *tawaaf*]?[6]

Response: The *tawaaf* around the *Ka'bah* is an act from the acts of worship, and the basis for all acts of worship is practicing restraint [until authentic evidence exists to support its permissibility].

It has been established on the authority of the Messenger of Allaah (*sal-Allaahu 'alayhe wa sallam*) that he used to utter the *takbeer* every time he passed *al-Hajar al-Aswad*. Obviously, one passes *al-Hajar al-Aswad* after having completed the seventh circuit, so it is legislated for him to utter the *takbeer* just as it was legislated for him to utter the *takbeer* at the beginning of each circuit whilst facing *al-Hajar al-Aswad*, and this being in accordance [with the practice of] the Messenger of Allaah (*sal-Allaahu 'alayhe wa sallam*) - by touching *al-Hajar al-Aswad* and kissing it if possible.

And with Allaah lies all success and may Allaah send prayers and salutations upon our Prophet (*sal-Allaahu 'alayhe wa sallam*) and his family and his Companions.

The Permanent Committee for Islaamic Research and Verdicts

5. Congregational prayer starts during Tawaaf or Sa'ee

Question: If the prayer starts whilst he is performing *tawaaf* or *sa'ee*,

---

6 Fataawa al-Lajnah ad-Daa.imah lil-Buhooth al-'Ilmiyyah wal-Iftaa. - Volume 11, Page 224, Question 1 of Fatwa No.2232.

what should he do?[7]

Response: If the prayer starts whilst he is performing *tawaaf* or *sa'ee*, he must join the congregation [in prayer]. And when the prayer finishes, he continues the [*tawaaf* or *sa'ee*] circuit [or lap] from where he stopped [for the prayer], and he is not required to start that particular circuit [or lap] from anew.

[For example], if it happened that the prayer starts and he is in the middle of the third lap of the *sa'ee*, then he must stop where he is and [join the congregation in] prayer [from where he has stopped]; And when the congregational prayer finishes, he continues his *sa'ee* from where he had stopped.

[Alternatively], if there is no-one around him [in the *mas'aa*] to pray [in congregation] with, he must leave the *mas'aa* and move forward [towards the *Ka'bah*] until he finds someone to pray [in congregation] with; And when the congregational prayer finishes, he returns to the *mas'aa* and continues with the lap from the spot where he left. And [in this case] he is not required to begin the lap from the beginning. Likewise we say regarding the *tawaaf*; If [for example] the prayer starts and you are near *al-Hijr* [Ismaa'eel], then you pray at the spot where you are. And when the congregational prayer finishes, you complete the circuit from the spot where you stopped [to join the congregational prayer] - and there is no need to repeat the circuit from anew from *al-Hajar al-Aswad*.

Shaykh Muhammad ibn 'Uthaymeen

---

7 Fataawa al-Hajj wal-'Umrah - Page 55.

6. Cutting hair from around the bottom of the head only

Question: During *hajj*, we see some [male] pilgrims cutting short their hair just from the bottom and around their heads only, leaving the rest of the head untouched. They don't cut any of the hair from there. When we told them that cutting the hair should be done equally from all over the head, they said [as a minimum] this is what is required. So, which of the two actions is obligatory?[8]

Response: That which is obligatory is for the head to either be shaved, or the hair [to be] cut equally from all over the head during *hajj* and *'umrah*. It is not required to take from every single hair. That which has been mentioned [in the question] is not sufficient according to the correct opinions of the people of knowledge and nor is it from the *Sunnah* of Muhammed (*sal-Allaahu 'alayhe wa sallam*)

And with Allaah lies all success and may Allaah send prayers and salutations upon our Prophet (*sal-Allaahu 'alayhe wa sallam*) and his family and his Companions.

The Permanent Committee for Islaamic Research and Verdicts

7. Delaying Tawaaf al-Ifaadhah until Tawaaf al-Wadaa'

Question: Is it permissible to delay *tawaaf al-ifaadhah* until *tawaaf al-wadaa'*, and how about taking a break between the seven circuits [of the *tawaaf*] to drink some water or other than this?[9]

---

8 Fataawa al-Lajnah ad-Daa.imah lil-Buhooth al-'Ilmiyyah wal-Iftaa. - Volume 11, Page 217, Question 5 of Fatwa No.1734.

9 Fataawa al-Hajj wal-'Umrah waz-Ziyaarah - Page 83.

Response: It is permissible to delay *tawaaf al-ifaadhah* until *tawaaf al-wadaa'* for fear of the crowds and that which is similar to this. So, if he performs *tawaaf* when he is [due] to leave [Makkah] and makes the intention for [the *tawaaf*, both] the *ifaadhah* and *wadaa'*, then this suffices for the two. He [must] then [promptly] depart [from Makkah] such that he remains true to his last act being the *tawaaf* around the House (*Ka'bah*).

However, it is better if *tawaaf al-ifaadhah* was done on the day of 'Eed [*al-Adh.haa*] or the days of *tashreeq*[10]. That said, he is permitted to delay this [as mentioned above].

As for [taking] a break between the circuits [of the *tawaaf*], then it is permissible so long as it is for something minor such as re-doing the *wudhoo*, drinking water, or performing the obligatory prayer or the funeral prayer, and that which is similar to this. However, if the break is half an hour (30 minutes) long or more, then the correct [opinion] is that [the circuits] which have preceded are nullified; So after this [long] break, he is required to resume the *tawaaf* by starting anew - from the beginning.

Shaykh 'Abdullaah ibn Jibreen

8. Detained from completing the Hajj or the 'Umrah

Question: If a pilgrim passed the *meeqaat*, uttering the *talbiyah* for *hajj* and *'umrah* without condition, and is then detained on account of illness or the like; What should he do if this [consequently] prevents him

---

10 The 11th, 12th and 13th days of Dhul-Hijjah.

from completing his [pilgrimage] rites?[11]

Response: Such a person is treated as *muh.sar* (detained). If he did not utter a condition, and thereafter an accident took place which prevented him from proceeding with his [pilgrimage] rites, he should then bear it and be patient if possible until the effects of the accident subside; [Only] then should he proceed with his [pilgrimage] rites. If he is unable to do this, then according to the correct opinion - he is considered as 'detained'. Allaah says about a detained person:

$$فَإِنْ أُحْصِرْتُمْ فَمَا اسْتَيْسَرَ مِنَ الْهَدْيِ$$

But if you are prevented from completing it, send an offering for sacrifice such as you may find[12]

According to the correct opinion, the case of being *muh.sar* occurs by way of an enemy, and sometimes occurs by other than an enemy. So, he should sacrifice an animal, shave or cut some of his hair, then take off his *ihraam*. This is the verdict for a *muh.sar*. He slaughters his sacrificial animal in the same place where he is detained, whether he is in the *Haram* (sacred) area or outside the *Haram*. If he does not find any poor people there, the meat should be carried to the poor inside the *Haram* area, or it should be carried to some other villages. After that, he should shave [his head] or have a haircut and then take off the *ihraam*. If he is unable to sacrifice an animal, he is required to fast for ten days, and then shave [his head] or have a haircut and then take off the *ihraam*.

Shaykh 'Abdul-'Azeez ibn Baaz

---

11 Fataawa Muhimmah tata'allaq bil-Hajj wal-'Umrah - Page 15, Fatwa No.3.

12 The Noble Qur.aan - Soorah al-Baqarah, Aayah 196.

111

9. Performing Tawaaf al-Ifaadhah after day of 'Eed

Question: A man heard it is permissible to perform *sa'ee* before *tawaaf* [*al-ifaadhah*], so he performed *sa'ee* and then *tawaaf* [*al-ifaadhah*] on the 12th or 13th day [of *Dhul-Hijjah*]. [Afterwards] he was told that this is specific to the day of 'Eed [*al-Adh.haa*][13]. So, what is the ruling [concerning this]?[14]

Response: That which is correct is there is no difference between the day of 'Eed and any other [day], in that it is permissible to perform *sa'ee* before *tawaaf*, even if this was after the day of 'Eed. The general [purport of the *hadeeth*] is that a man said to the Prophet (*sal-Allaahu 'alayhe wa sallam*): 'I have performed *sa'ee* before *tawaaf*'. And He (*sal-Allaahu 'alayhe wa sallam*) replied:

«[there is] no harm [in having done so]»[15]

And since the *hadeeth* was general, there is no difference between [performing] that on the day of 'Eed or on [any of the days] which follow.

Shaykh Muhammad ibn 'Uthaymeen

10. Entering Hijr Ismaa'eel whilst making the Tawaaf

Question: Is it permissible for the *hajj* or *'umrah* pilgrim to enter *Hijr*

---

13 The 10th day of Dhul-Hijjah.

14 Fataawa al-Hajj wal-'Umrah waz-Ziyaarah - Page 91.

15 Sunan Abee Daawood/2015, Saheeh Ibn Khuzaymah/2774, Sunan ad-Daarimee/ 2565.

Ismaa'eel whilst performing *tawaaf*?[16]

Response: It is not permissible for the *hajj* or the *'umrah* pilgrim to enter *Hijr* Ismaa'eel whilst performing *tawaaf* of the House (*Ka'bah*), even during the voluntary *tawaaf*.

He will not rewarded for that if he does so, because *tawaaf* is required around the House and the *Hijr* is part of the House, for that which Al-laah (*Subhaanahu wa Ta'aala*) says:

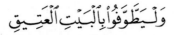

and perform tawaaf around the ancient House[17]

Also, that which is narrated by Muslim and others on the authority of 'Aa'ishah (*radhi-yallaahu 'anhaa*) who said: I asked the Messenger of Allaah (*sal-Allaahu 'alayhe wa sallam*) regarding the *Hijr* and he said:

«it is part of the House»[18]

And in another wording, she said: I vowed to pray inside the House and he (*sal-Allaahu 'alayhe wa sallam*) said:

«pray in the Hijr, for certainly the Hijr is part of the House...»[19]

---

16   Fataawa al-Lajnah ad-Daa.imah lil-Buhooth al-'Ilmiyyah wal-Iftaa. - Volume 11, Page 233, Question 1 of Fatwa No.1775;
Fataawa al-Hajj wal-'Umrah waz-Ziyaarah - Page 77.

17   The Noble Qur.aan - Soorah al-Hajj, Aayah 29.

18   Sunan Abee Daawood/1875, Musannaf 'Abdur-Razzaaq/8941, as-Sunan al-Kubraa lil-Bayhaqee/9314.

19   Sharh Ma'aanee al-Aathaar lit-Tahaawee/2300.

And with Allaah lies all success and may Allaah send prayers and salutations upon our Prophet (*sal-Allaahu 'alayhe wa sallam*) and his family and his Companions.

The Permanent Committee for Islaamic Research and Verdicts

11. Forgetfully left four laps of the Sa'ee

Question: A man performed *'umrah* and forgetfully or ignorantly left four laps [of the total seven laps] of the *sa'ee*; So what is he required to do?[20]

Response: He is required to perform the remaining [four] laps [of the *sa'ee*] to complete the [full total of] seven, whether this [error] occurred during *hajj* or *'umrah*. Even if he had travelled [back] to his home, he is [now] required to return to Makkah and perform the laps he left in order to complete his *'umrah*. [Until he returns to complete the outstanding *sa'ee* laps, during this period] he is considered to be in *ihraam* which prevents him from engaging [in sexual intercourse] with his wife until he completes his *'umrah*.

Shaykh 'Abdul-'Azeez ibn Baaz

12. Wudhoo when performing the Tawaaf and the Sa'ee

Question: Is it compulsory to be in a state of *wudhoo* in order to perform *tawaaf* and *sa'ee*?[21]

---

20 Fataawa al-Hajj wal-'Umrah waz-Ziyaarah - Page 131-132.

21 Fataawa al-Hajj wal-'Umrah waz-Ziyaarah - Page 78.

Response: Being in a state of *wudhoo* is compulsory for *tawaaf* only. As for *sa'ee*, then it is better to be in a state of *wudhoo*, however, if not, then it is acceptable.

Shaykh 'Abdul-'Azeez ibn Baaz

13. Jogging from Safaa to Marwaa & from Marwah to Safaa

Question: Jogging whilst performing *sa'ee* is done when proceeding from *Safaa* to *Marwah*, and is it also done on the way back to *Safaa* [from *Marwah*]?[22]

Response: Yes. It is done on the way from *Marwah* to *Safaa*, as it is done on the way from *Safaa* to *Marwah*; In accordance with the practice of the Messenger of Allaah which is confirmed in the authenticated *ahaadeeth*.

8

And with Allaah lies all success and may Allaah send prayers and salutations upon our Prophet (*sal-Allaahu 'alayhe wa sallam*) and his family and his Companions.

The Permanent Committee for Islaamic Research and Verdicts

14. Performed Sa'ee but did not shave or cut hair

Question: A pilgrim performing the *tamattu' hajj* performed *tawaaf* and *sa'ee*, then changed into his normal clothes, but did not shave or cut his hair. Later, after *hajj*, he asked about this and was informed he

---

22 Fataawa al-Lajnah ad-Daa.imah lil-Buhooth al-'Ilmiyyah wal-Iftaa. - Volume 11, Page 258, Question 6 of Fatwa No.2757.

had made a mistake. What is he now required to do since the time for *hajj* has passed?[23]

Response: This pilgrim is considered as one who has neglected an obligatory act from the obligatory acts of *'umrah* [and *hajj*] - that being either shaving or cutting the hair. According to the people of knowledge, he is required to make a sacrifice as expiation and distribute [the meat] to the poor and needy in Makkah and [the validity of] his *hajj* is not affected.

Shaykh Muhammad ibn 'Uthaymeen

15. Unable to depart from Makkah after Tawaaf al-Wadaa'

Question: A man performing *hajj*, performed *tawaaf al-wadaa'* at night but was unable to leave Makkah after the *tawaaf*, so remained in Makkah until the morning when he travelled. What is the ruling [in this situation]?[24]

Response: It is legislated for *tawaaf al-wadaa'* to be performed just before his departure from Makkah, as occurs in the *hadeeth* of Ibn 'Abbaas (*radhi-yAllaahu 'anhumaa*) whose authenticity is agreed upon:

«The people have been commanded that their last act (before departure) should be (tawaaf) around the House (Ka'bah) except for the menstruating

---

23 Fataawa al-Hajj wal-'Umrah waz-Ziyaarah - Page 93.

24 Fataawa al-Hajj wal-'Umrah waz-Ziyaarah - Page 84.

***woman*»[25]**

So, as long as he performed *tawaaf* [*al-wadaa'*] with the intention to depart at night, but was unable to do so until morning, there is nothing required of him in [regard to] that, *inshaa.-Allaah*. And if he were to repeat the *tawaaf* [*al-wadaa'*] before [actually] departing, then this is better.

And with Allaah lies all success and may Allaah send prayers and salutations upon our Prophet (*sal-Allaahu 'alayhe wa sallam*) and his family and his Companions.

The Permanent Committee for Islaamic Research and Verdicts

16. Making long supplication at beginning of Tawaaf

Question: When approaching the line[26] placed as a sign for the beginning of the *tawaaf* [in line with *al-Hajar al-Aswad*], some pilgrims stand there for a long time preventing the[ir] brothers [and sisters] from proceeding with their *tawaaf*. So, what is the ruling regarding standing on this line and making a long supplication?[27]

Response: Standing on this line for a long period is not required, rather, the person should face *al-Hajar al-Aswad* and make a sign [with the palm of the right hand] towards it and recite *Allaahu-Akbar* and then

---

25 Saheeh al-Bukhaaree/1755, Saheeh Muslim/380, Musannaf Ibn Abee Shaybah/13600, Saheeh ibn Khuzaymah/2999, Sunan ad-Daaraqutnee/2786.

26 This line has now been removed, yet many pilgrims continue to congregate along this area making long supplications.

27 Daleel al-Akhtaa.a yaqa'a feehaa al-Haaj wal-Mu'tamir wat-tahdtheer minhaa - Page 42.

proceed, since this is not a place to stand for a long time. However, I see some people standing and saying: 'I have made the intention for the Sake of Allaah, the Almighty, to perform seven circuits [of the *Ka'bah*] or *tawaaf* for *'umrah*, or voluntary *tawaaf*', or that which is similar to this. This is a mistake in the [manner the] intention [is made], since we have [previously] warned that making a verbal intention in acts of worship is an innovation, which has not been mentioned on the authority of the Prophet (*sal-Allaahu 'alayhe wa sallam*) nor any of his Companions (*radhi-yAllaahu 'anhum*). So you must perform your acts of worship for the Sake of Allaah (*Subhaanahu wa Ta'aala*) and He has [complete] knowledge of your intention, so there is no need to verbally do so.

Shaykh Muhammad ibn 'Uthaymeen

17. Not shaving or cutting hair equally from all over head

Question: What is the ruling if the *hajj* and *'umrah* pilgrim cuts his hair short from only the sides of his head, without equally [cutting his hair] from all over his head, and thereafter removing his *ihraam*?[28]

Response: The ruling is that if this occurred during *hajj*, and he had already performed *tawaaf* and stoned [the *jamaraat* pillars], then he should remain in his [normal] clothing and complete the shaving or shortening of the hair on his head. If, however, this occurred during *'umrah*, then he is required to remove his [normal] clothing and return to [wearing] the *ihraam* garment and then shave or shorten the hair equally from all over his head - and this is to be done whilst he is wearing the *ihraam* garment.

Shaykh Muhammad ibn 'Uthaymeen

---

28 Fataawa al-Hajj wal-'Umrah waz-Ziyaarah - Page 93.

18. Performed the Sa'ee before the Tawaaf

Question: Is it permissible to perform *sa'ee* before *tawaaf*, whether it be during *hajj* or *'umrah*?[29]

Response: [It is from] the *Sunnah* [that] *tawaaf* be [performed] first, and then *sa'ee* after it. And if out of ignorance he performed *sa'ee* before *tawaaf*, then there is no harm in that, as it has been established that a man said to the Prophet (*sal-Allaahu 'alayhe wa sallam*): 'I have performed *sa'ee* before *tawaaf*'. [And] He (*sal-Allaahu 'alayhe wa sallam*) responded:

«[there is] no harm [in having done so]»[30]

And this suggests that if *sa'ee* is performed before *tawaaf*, then it suffices; However, it is from the *Sunnah* to perform *tawaaf* and then *sa'ee* [after it] - that is the *Sunnah*, both during *'umrah* and *hajj*.

Shaykh 'Abdul-'Azeez ibn Baaz

19. Performing Sa'ee without Wudhoo and Adhaan is called

Question: Bearing in mind the permissibility of performing *sa'ee* without *wudhoo*, if the call to prayer is made whilst he is performing *sa'ee* between *Safaa* and *Marwah* - should he leave the *Haram* (*masjid*) in order to perform *wudhoo* and [then] return to pray in congregation, and thereafter complete the *sa'ee* or is he required to start from the

---

29 Fataawa al-Hajj wal-'Umrah waz-Ziyaarah - Page 90.

30 Sunan Abee Daawood/2015, Saheeh Ibn Khuzaymah/2774, Sunan ad-Daarimee/ 2565.

beginning?[31]

Response: Yes. He must leave the *Haram* (*masjid*) to go to the washroom to perform *wudhoo* and [return to] pray with the congregation. In this situation, if there is a lengthy delay, then he is required to begin *sa'ee* anew, and if there is only a short delay, then he is not required to begin *sa'ee* anew.

Let us consider if the *wudhoo* washroom is near the *mas'aa* and [therefore] does not take much time, and that by the time he returns [from having performed *wudhoo*] the prayer starts - this is [considered as] a short time - in which case he can complete the *sa'ee* [from where he left off].

If, however, the time was lengthy, then [in this case] he must start the *sa'ee* from the beginning (i.e. from the first lap at *Safaa*).

Shaykh Muhammad ibn 'Uthaymeen

20. Performing the Tawaaf or engaging in prayer

Question: Is it better to repeatedly perform *tawaaf* or [engage] in voluntary prayer?[32]

Response: There is a difference of opinion regarding which [of the two acts] is more preferable, however, that which is better [to do] is to combine the two [acts]; So increase [in engaging] in [voluntary] prayer as well as performing *tawaaf* so as to combine the good of the two [acts].

---

31 Fataawa al-Hajj wal-'Umrah - Page 56.

32 Fataawa al-Hajj wal-'Umrah waz-Ziyaarah - Page 88.

With respect to the foreigners (visitors), some of the people of knowledge recommend [the performance of] *tawaaf* because they do not have the *Ka'bah* in their lands, [therefore] so long as they are in Makkah - it is preferable they increase in [performing] *tawaaf*; Whereas others recommend [engaging in] prayer because it is better. However, regarding these two [acts], I am of the opinion it is more preferable to increase in doing them both - even if he is a foreigner (visitor) so [that] he does not miss out on the excellence of either of the two.

Shaykh 'Abdul-'Azeez ibn Baaz

21. Performing the Tawaaf right away

Question: If I intended [to perform] *'umrah* or *hajj*, and [thereby] assumed the state of *ihraam* and entered *al-Masjid al-Haraam*, should I pray the two *rak'ah*s of *tahiyyatul-masjid*, or should I begin my *tawaaf* right away?[33]

Response: That which is legislated for *hajj 'umrah* pilgrims upon entering *al-Masjid al-Haraam* is to begin with the *tawaaf*, and the two *rak'ah*s they pray after the *tawaaf* [behind *maqaam* Ibraaheem] will suffice the [two *rak'ah*s of] *tahiyyatul-masjid*. If, however, there is a legislated reason preventing him from [beginning] the *tawaaf* upon entering the *Masjid*, then he should pray two *rak'ah*s of *tahiyyatul-masjid*, and then perform *tawaaf* when that is easy for him. And likewise, if he entered the *Masjid* and the [congregational] prayer had just begun, then he should pray with the people [in congregation] and then perform *tawaaf* after that.

---

33 ad-Durar an-Naadhirah fil-Fataawa al-Mu'aasirah - Page 394-395.

And Allaah is the Expounder of all success.

Shaykh 'Abdul-'Azeez ibn Baaz

22. Voluntary prayers, Tawaaf and reciting Qur.aan

Question: Which is better to perform in *al-Masjid al-Haraam* during *Ramadhaan*: supererogatory prayers, *tawaaf* or reciting the *Qur.aan*?[34]

Response: *Tawaaf* is preferable for the non-Makkans, because it is not always easy for them [to travel to Makkah] to do so. As for the people of Makkah [themselves], then it is preferable [for them] to perform supererogatory prayers and recite [the *Qur.aan*] so long as the time is appropriate[35]. However, if the *tawaaf* is difficult for the visitor [to Makkah], or there exists something which prevents him from performing *tawaaf* such as congestion and many women, in addition to the fear of [falling into] *fitnah*, then the supererogatory prayers are better. It is also possible to combine between performing *tawaaf*, reciting [the *Qur. aan*], and supplicating [to Allaah], and [in so doing] attaining double the reward, and Allaah knows best.

Shaykh 'Abdullaah ibn Jibreen

23. Taking a break from performing the Tawaaf or the Sa'ee

Question: Is the pilgrim required to take a break from performing *tawaaf* or *sa'ee* in order to perform the prayer?[36]

---

34 Fataawa as-Siyaam libni Jibreen - Page 175, Fatwa No.192.

35 i.e. not praying during the prohibited times of after Fajr, at Zawaal and after 'Asr.

36 Fataawa al-Hajj wal-'Umrah - Page 56.

Response: If the prayer is obligatory, then it is obligatory for him to take a break from performing *tawaaf* or *sa'ee* so he can perform the prayer. That is because the congregational prayer is obligatory, and [in this case] one is permitted to take a break from [performing *tawaaf* and] *sa'ee* because of it.

So his taking a break from performing *sa'ee* or *tawaaf* is considered a permissible break, whilst his joining the congregation[al prayer] is considered obligatory - [in which case] it is obligatory for him to join the congregation[al prayer].

However, if it was a voluntary prayer, such as the *taraaweeh* night prayer in *Ramadhaan*, then it is known one is not [allowed] to take a break from performing *sa'ee* or *tawaaf* because of it.

[That said] it is better he makes enquiries [about the timing] and performs *tawaaf* or *sa'ee* after the night prayer or before it, so that he does not miss out on the excellence of the night prayer in congregation.

Shaykh Muhammad ibn 'Uthaymeen

24. Tawaaf & Sa'ee once the obligatory prayer begins

Question: What is the ruling regarding the one performing *hajj* or *'umrah*, and when the obligatory prayer begins, he has not [yet] completed the *tawaaf* or *sa'ee*?[37]

Response: He should pray with the congregation, then continue his *tawaaf* or *sa'ee* from where he had stopped [just before the prayer]. So

---

37 Fataawa al-Hajj wal-'Umrah waz-Ziyaarah - Page 80.

he starts from [the point] where he stopped.

Shaykh 'Abdul-'Azeez ibn Baaz

25. The manner of clinging on to the Ka'bah

Question: What is the manner in which one should cling onto the *Ka'bah* between *al-Hajar al-Aswad* and the door?[38]

Response: Clinging on to the *Ka'bah* is done by standing [between *al-Hajar al-Aswad* and the door] and placing the hands, arms and cheeks upon the wall.

Shaykh Muhammad ibn 'Uthaymeen

26. The Tawaaf and Sa'ee of one being carried

Question: Regarding the one who is performing *sa'ee* or *tawaaf* carrying a small child or someone who is ill; Does the *sa'ee* and *tawaaf* suffice both of them - the carrier and the one being carried or not?[39]

Response: It suffices them both - based upon the intention of the carrier, and the one being carried being of sound mind; This is the most correct of the two opinions of the scholars.

And with Allaah lies all success and may Allaah send prayers and saluta-

---

38 Daleel al-Akhtaa.a yaqa'a feehaa al-Haaj wal-Mu'tamir wat-tahdtheer minhaa - Page 44;
Fataawa al-Hajj wal-'Umrah - Page 59.

39 Fataawa al-Hajj wal-'Umrah waz-Ziyaarah - Page 76.

tions upon our Prophet (*sal-Allaahu 'alayhe wa sallam*) and his family and his Companions.

The Permanent Committee for Islaamic Research and Verdicts

27. The two Rak'ahs behind Maqaam Ibraaheem

Question: Is it compulsory to pray the two *rak'ahs* for the *tawaaf* behind *maqaam* Ibraaheem, and what is the ruling regarding one who forgets this?[40]

Response: It is not compulsory to pray two *rak'ahs* behind *maqaam* Ibraaheem, rather it is acceptable in any place in the *Haram* (*al-Masjid al-Haraam*). Whoever forgets to pray them, then there is no harm because they are recommended and not obligatory.

And Allaah is the Expounder of success.

Shaykh 'Abdul-'Azeez ibn Baaz

28. Unsure as to whether I had passed wind during Tawaaf

Question: During *tawaaf al-wadaa'*, after I had performed five circuits around the *Ka'bah* I felt some motion in my backside; *Iblees* began whispering to me that I had passed wind, but I did not pay any attention to this whispering because I did not feel that I had passed any wind. Since I had completely lost the sense of smell, I sought refuge in Allaah and put my faith in Allaah and continued performing *tawaaf* and then [upon completion] performed the two *rak'ahs* [of prayer]. So what is your

---

40 Fataawa al-Hajj wal-'Umrah waz-Ziyaarah - Page 81.

advice to me in this case, and am I liable for any penalty?[41]

Response: The basic rule is that you remain in the state of purification, as the occurrence of doubt as to whether you passed wind does not nullify your state of purification [until you are absolutely sure], so your *tawaaf* and your prayer afterwards is correct/sound, [*inshaa.-Allaah*].

And with Allaah lies all success and may Allaah send prayers and salutations upon our Prophet (*sal-Allaahu 'alayhe wa sallam*) and his family and his Companions.

The Permanent Committee for Islaamic Research and Verdicts

29. Woman uncovering face whilst performing Tawaaf

Question: Is it permissible for a woman performing *hajj* or *'umrah* to uncover her face whilst performing *tawaaf* around the *Ka'bah*, in the presence of non-*mahram* men?[42]

Response: The face of the woman is an *'awrah* and it is not permissible to uncover it in front of non-*mahram* men, not during the *tawaaf* and nor during other than it, and nor whether she is in the state of *ihraam* or not. So, if she performed *tawaaf* having uncovered her face, then she has committed a sin by uncovering her face, but her *tawaaf* is correct/sound. However, she should cover it with other than a *niqaab* if she is in the state of *ihraam*.

---

41 Fataawa al-Lajnah ad-Daa.imah lil-Buhooth al-'Ilmiyyah wal-Iftaa. - Volume 11, Page 244, Question No.4 of Fatwa No.11935.

42 Fataawa al-Lajnah ad-Daa.imah lil-Buhooth al-'Ilmiyyah wal-Iftaa. - Volume 11, Page 193, Question 1 of Fatwa No.4151.

And with Allaah lies all success and may Allaah send prayers and salutations upon our Prophet (*sal-Allaahu 'alayhe wa sallam*) and his family and his Companions.

The Permanent Committee for Islaamic Research and Verdicts

30. Women crowding amongst men at Safaa and Marwah

Question: From that which is known is that *Safaa* is small and *Marwah* is smaller. However, we see [some] women ascending upon *Safaa* and *Marwah* and crowd amongst the men. Is it from the *Sunnah* for the women to ascend upon *Safaa* [and *Marwah*]?[43]

Response: That which is known according to the jurists, is that it is not recommended for the women to ascend upon *Safaa* and [nor] *Marwah*. Instead, they should stand at the foot of each mount, then move on to complete the remaining laps. However, it may be that these women who were seen ascending *Safaa* and *Marwah* are with their *mahrams*. It is not recommended for them to split up from their *mahrams* because of the fear they may lose each other, otherwise, that which is better is for the woman is not to gather amongst the men in any situation that does not require so.

Shaykh Muhammad ibn 'Uthaymeen

31. Women jogging between two green lights during Sa'ee

Question: Regarding women jogging between the two green [lights]

---

43 Daleel al-Akhtaa.a yaqa'a feehaa al-Haaj wal-Mu'tamir wat-tahdtheer minhaa - Page 56.

during *sa'ee*, in my limited readings through the books of *fiqh* in the chapters pertaining to *hajj* and *'umrah*, I have not found anything to suggest women should not jog. I once heard one of the scholars on television say that women should not jog during *sa'ee*, rather it is specific to the men only; This is because it is more protective for the woman, so she does not reveal her beauty and that which would cause *fitnah* if she were to jog. However, he did not mention any evidence for his opinion. So I said to myself, if my opinion is correct from his judicial reasoning, then the jogging is also a *Sunnah* which Haajar[44] started, however, and all praise is due to Allaah [alone], I understand the [Shaykh's] opinion, that the religion is not based upon [unqualified] opinions, as the *Ameer al-Mu.mineen* 'Alee (*radhi-yAllaahu 'anhu*) said. Please advice us, and may Allaah bless you, since I take my family for *'umrah* from time to time and we need to know that which is correct regarding this issue?[45]

Response: Ibn al-Munthir said:

'The people of knowledge are in agreement that there is no jogging for the women around the House (*Ka'bah*), and nor [during *sa'ee*] between [the green lights of] *Safaa* and *Marwah*, and nor are they to place the *ridaa* (top part of the *ihraam*) under their right armpits; This is because the principle behind the two is to show stamina and hardiness, and that is not meant for the women, because what is meant for the women is to cover themselves, and since the jogging involves placing the *ridaa* (top part of the *ihraam*) under their right armpits then this leads to displaying [the woman's beauty] and revealing [her charms].'

---

44 Wife of Prophet Ibraaheem ('alayhis-salaam).

45 Fataawa al-Lajnah ad-Daa.imah lil-Buhooth al-'Ilmiyyah wal-Iftaa. - Volume 11, Page 226, Question 5 of Fatwa No.8820.

And with Allaah lies all success and may Allaah send prayers and salutations upon our Prophet (*sal-Allaahu 'alayhe wa sallam*) and his family and his Companions.

The Permanent Committee for Islaamic Research and Verdicts

Chapter Nine

Staying in Minaa

1. In Minaa until midnight then leaves for Makkah and does not return until after Fajr

Question: What is the ruling regarding one who remains in Minaa until midnight, then leaves for Makkah and does not return until after *Fajr*?[1]

Response: If the time is midnight, then that is the middle of the night in Minaa and in that case there is no harm in leaving Minaa after this time, even though it is better to remain in Minaa [for the duration of] the day and night. However, if the time of midnight occurs before the middle of the night[2], then do not leave because the condition for remaining in Minaa is to spend most of the night there as has been mentioned by our jurists, may Allaah (*Subhaanahu wa Ta'aala*) have Mercy upon them.

Shaykh Muhammad ibn 'Uthaymeen

---

1 Fataawa al-Hajj wal-'Umrah waz-Ziyaarah - Page 104.

2 Briefly, the middle of the night is estimated between the time of maghrib and fajr the following morning; So if maghrib occurs at 7pm and fajr occurs at 6am, then the middle of the night will be calculated as the time between 7pm and 6am which is 12:30am.

2. Made haste and left Minaa after second day of stoning

Question: If a pilgrim leaves Minaa before sunset on the 12th [of *Dhul-Hijjah* - the second day of stoning] with the intention to legally make haste [and thereby legally miss the third day of stoning] and later intends to return to Minaa for work after sunset, will he still be regarded as one who has legally made haste [by only completing 2 days of stoning]?[3]

Response: Yes, he will be regarded as one who has legally made haste, because he has completed the *hajj* and his intention to return to Minaa for work does not affect this position because he has made the intention to return for work which he has been entrusted with and not to continue with the [*hajj*] rituals.

Shaykh Muhammad ibn 'Uthaymeen

3. Not permitted to spend the night in Minaa

Question: What is the ruling regarding the pilgrim whose work commitments do not permit him to spend the night in Minaa during the days of *tashreeq*[4]?[5]

Response: [The requirement to] spend the night in Minaa is waived for those who have a legally valid reason [not to do so]. However, they are required to seize any opportunity to spend the rest of the time [outside of work commitments] in Minaa with the pilgrims.

Shaykh 'Abdul-'Azeez ibn Baaz

---

3 Fataawa al-Hajj wal-'Umrah waz-Ziyaarah - Page 107.

4 The 11th, 12th and 13th days Dhul-Hijjah.

5 Fataawa al-Hajj wal-'Umrah waz-Ziyaarah - Page 105.

4. Spending the entire night in Minaa is better

Question: Allaah granted me the *towfeeq* to perform the *hajj* with my husband, and during the three days of *tashreeq*[6] we only spent [part of the night] in Minaa until 1am and then returned to Makkah where we had a house; So is this permissible? Please advise us and may Allaah reward you with good.[7]

Response: Spending most of the night in Minaa is sufficient, and all praise is due to Allaah [alone], neither of you are liable for any penalty. However, if you were to have remained in Minaa the entire night, following the example of the Prophet (*sal-Allaahu 'alayhe wa sallam*) and his Companions (*radhi-yAllaahu 'anhum*), that would have been better.

And with Allaah lies all Success.

Shaykh 'Abdul-'Azeez ibn Baaz

5. Spending the nights of 11th, 12th & 13th outside Minaa

Question: What is the ruling regarding spending the nights outside Minaa during the days of *tashreeq*[8] - whether it was done intentionally or due to being unable to find a resting place therein? And when is the pilgrim permitted to [finally] depart from Minaa?[9]

---

6 The 11th, 12th and 13th days Dhul-Hijjah.

7 Fataawa al-Hajj wal-'Umrah waz-Ziyaarah - Page 104.

8 The 11th, 12th and 13th days Dhul-Hijjah.

9 Fataawa al-Hajj wal-'Umrah waz-Ziyaarah - Page 105.

Response: According to the correct opinion [in this matter], it is obligatory to remain in Minaa on the night of the 11th[10] and the night of the 12th[11]; This is what the researchers from the people of knowledge have suggested is the preponderant opinion [in this matter] concerning both the male and female pilgrims. And if they are unable to find a resting place, then they are excused [of this obligation] and as such they are not liable for any penalty. Whoever spends the night outside Minaa without a [legally valid] reason, then they are required to offer a sacrifice [by slaughtering a sheep and distributing its meat to the poor and needy of the people of Makkah].

Shaykh 'Abdul-'Azeez ibn Baaz

6. Unable to find place in Minaa during days of Tashreeq

Question: What is the ruling regarding those performing *hajj* being unable to find a place to rest in Minaa for the days of *tashreeq*[12]?[13]

Response: If they were unable to find a place to rest in Minaa, then they should proceed to the furthest tents of the pilgrims [on the outskirts], even if they are beyond the limits of Minaa as Allaah (*Subhaanahu wa Ta'ala*) has said:

$$\text{فَٱتَّقُوا۟ ٱللَّهَ مَا ٱسۡتَطَعۡتُمۡ}$$

So keep your duty to Allaah and fear Him as much

---

10 The 10th day of Dhul-Hijjah.

11 The 11th day of Dhul-Hijjah.

12 The 11th, 12th and 13th days Dhul-Hijjah.

13 Fataawa al-Hajj wal-'Umrah waz-Ziyaarah - Page 103.

as you can[14]

Shaykh Muhammad ibn 'Uthaymeen

---

14 The Noble Qur.aan - Soorah at-Taghaabun, Aayah 16.

Chapter Ten

Spending the day in 'Arafah

1. Departed from 'Arafah before sunset due to work

<u>Question</u>: What is the ruling regarding one who performed the *hajj* and then departed from 'Arafah before sunset due to his work commitments?[1]

<u>Response</u>: According to the majority of the People of Knowledge, the one who departed from 'Arafah before sunset is required to make *fidyah* (pay a ransom), except if he were able to return there during the night, in which case the *fidyah* is not required. And the *fidyah* is to slaughter a sheep and distribute its meat to the poor and needy in Makkah.

Shaykh 'Abdul-'Azeez ibn Baaz

2. Referring to Jabal 'Arafah as Jabal ar-Rahmah

<u>Question</u>: They call *Jabal 'Arafah* (Mount of 'Arafah) *Jabal ar-Rahmah*

---

1 Fataawa al-Hajj wal-'Umrah waz-Ziyaarah, Page 96.

(Mount of Mercy), so what is the ruling regarding this name and is there any basis for this?[2]

Response: I do not know of any basis for this name from the *Sunnah*, that the mount which is in 'Arafah upon which the Prophet (*sal-Allaahu 'alayhe wa sallam*) stood is called *Jabal ar-Rahmah*. If there is no basis for it in the *Sunnah* then it is not befitting to apply this [name] to it. [As for] those who have applied this name, then they have possibly observed this is a great [standing] place which is recognised as a place of Allaah's Forgiveness and Mercy for those standing upon it in 'Arafah; They therefore named it such. So that which is better is not to call it by this name, rather, call it *Jabal 'Arafah*, or the mount at which the Prophet (*sal-Allaahu 'alayhe wa sallam*) stood, or that which is similar to this.

Shaykh Muhammad ibn 'Uthaymeen

3. Spending the Day of 'Arafah outside 'Arafah

Question: If the pilgrim rests just outside the boundary of 'Arafah until sunest, and then departs from there [without actually entering 'Arafah itself], what is the ruling?[3]

Response: If the pilgrim did not rest in 'Arafah during the [legislated] time he is required [to be in 'Arafah], then his *hajj* is invalidated as the Prophet (*sal-Allaahu 'alayhe wa sallam*) said:

---

2 Daleel al-Akhtaa.a yaqa'a feehaa al-Haaj wal-Mu'tamir wat-tahdtheer minhaa - Page 69;
    Fataawa al-Hajj wal-'Umrah - Page 60.

3 Fataawa al-Hajj wal-'Umrah waz-Ziyaarah - Page 96.

«The hajj is 'Arafah; So whoever gets to 'Arafah [even] during the night - before the onset of Fajr, then he has attained the hajj»[4]

And the time [period] he is required to be in 'Arafah is from after *zawaal* on the day of 'Arafah[5] until the arrival of *Fajr* the following morning of *'Eed*[6]. This is what the people of knowledge are unanimously agreed upon.

As for [being in 'Arafah during the time period] before *zawaal*, then therein is a difference of opinion amongst the people of knowledge; The majority are of the opinion it is not acceptable unless he enters 'Arafah after *zawaal* - even during the night. And whoever enters ['Arafah] after *zawaal* during the day or the night, then that is sufficient for him, [however] it is better to be there during the day - after [having performed] the *Zhuhr* and *'Asr* prayers in shortened form - until sunset.

Whoever is in 'Arafah during the day, then it is not permissible for him to depart before sunset; If he does so, then according to the majority of the people of knowledge he is required to offer a sacrifice [by slaughtering a sheep and distributing its meat to the poor and needy of the people of Makkah]. This is because he abandoned an obligatory act.

Shaykh 'Abdul-'Azeez ibn Baaz

---

4 Sunan Abee Daawood/1949, Sunan at-Tirmidhee/889, Sunan an-Nasaa.ee/3044, Saheeh Ibn Khuzaymah/2822.

5 The 9th day of Dhul-Hijjah.

6 The 10th day of Dhul-Hijjah.

4. The Day of 'Arafah falling on a Friday

Question: Some people say that if the day of 'Arafah[7] falls on a Friday, then the pilgrim is rewarded as if he has performed 7 *hajj*s. Is there any evidence from the *Sunnah* regarding this?[8]

Response: There is no authentic evidence confirming this. Some people [even] believe this equates to [having performed] 70 or 72 *hajj*s, and this is also incorrect.

And with Allaah lies all success and may Allaah send prayers and salutations upon our Prophet (*sal-Allaahu 'alayhe wa sallam*) and his family and his Companions.

The Permanent Committee for Islaamic Research and Verdicts

5. Visiting Jabal 'Arafah before or after Hajj

Question: Some pilgrims visit *Jabal 'Arafah* before performing the *hajj*, or afterwards, and pray upon it [at its peak]. What is the ruling regarding visiting *Jabal 'Arafah*, and what is the ruling regarding praying upon it?[9]

Response: Its ruling is as is known from the *Sharee'ah* ruling, and it is

---

7 The 9th day of Dhul-Hijjah.

8 Fataawa al-Lajnah ad-Daa.imah lil-Buhooth al-'Ilmiyyah wal-Iftaa. - Volume 11, Page 211, Question 3 of Fatwa No.7890.

9 Daleel al-Akhtaa.a yaqa'a feehaa al-Haaj wal-Mu'tamir wat-tahdtheer minhaa - Page 69;
Fataawa al-Hajj wal-'Umrah - Page 60-61.

that anyone who worships Allaah in a manner that has not been legislated, then he is an innovator. So it is known from this that he who has intended to pray on *Jabal 'Arafah* or at the bottom or just touch it or [anything] similar to this, then this is an innovation which is disliked and frowned upon. They should be told: There is nothing special about this mount except that it is from the *Sunnah* for a person to stand by the rocks on the day of 'Arafah[10], just as the Prophet (*sal-Allaahu 'alayhe wa sallam*) stood [by them]. The Prophet (*sal-Allaahu 'alayhe wa sallam*) stood by the rocks and said:

> *«I have stood here, however, all of 'Arafah is a standing place»*[11]

So based upon this, it is also not befitting for a person to impose hardship upon himself on the day of 'Arafah by going to the mount and quite possibly causing hardship for others. In doing so, he becomes tired from the heat and thirst, and thereby has sinned because he has imposed hardship in a matter which Allaah has not made obligatory for him.

Shaykh Muhammad ibn 'Uthaymeen

6. Voluntary prayers after Zhuhr and 'Asr

Question: Is it permissible for the one performing *hajj*, to perform voluntary prayers after having offered the *Zhuhr* and *'Asr* prayers with the

---

10 The 9th day of Dhul-Hijjah.

11 Saheeh Muslim.

imaam, on the day of 'Arafah[12] until the time of sunset?[13]

Response: The Messenger (*sal-Allaahu 'alayhe wa sallam*) did not perform any voluntary prayers on the day of 'Arafah, after having offered the
Zhuhr and *'Asr* prayers combined, and at the time of *Zhuhr*[14]. And if it
was legislated then he would have been more careful about performing
them than us, and good - all good is in adhering to following his *Sunnah*.

And with Allaah lies all success and may Allaah send prayers and salutations upon our Prophet (*sal-Allaahu 'alayhe wa sallam*) and his family
and his Companions.

The Permanent Committee for Islaamic Research and Verdicts

7. When to proceed to 'Arafah and when to depart

Question: When should the pilgrim proceed to 'Arafah, and when should
he depart from there?[15]

Response: It is legislated that he proceeds [to 'Arafah] after sunrise on
the day of 'Arafah which is the 9th day [of *Dhul-Hijjah*]; There, at the
time of *Zhuhr*, after one *adhaan* and two *iqaamah*s, he is required to
perform the *Zhuhr* and *'Asr* prayers combined and shortened - following

---

12 The 9th day of Dhul-Hijjah.

13 Fataawa al-Lajnah ad-Daa.imah lil-Buhooth al-'Ilmiyyah wal-Iftaa. - Volume 11, Page
    212, Question 3 of Fatwa No.7894.

14 Technically referred to as 'jam'u taqdeem'.

15 Fataawa al-Hajj wal-'Umrah waz-Ziyaarah - Page 95-96

the example of the Prophet (*sal-Allaahu 'alayhi wa sallam*) and his Companions (*radhi-yAllaahu 'anhum*).

He is required to remain [in 'Arafah] until sunset [all the time] busying himself with the remembrance of Allaah, supplication, and reciting the *Qur.aan*, as well as reciting the *talbiyah* until sunset. It is legislated that he increases in the recitation of:

$$ \text{«لاَ إِلَهَ إِلاَّ اللهُ وَحْدَهُ لاَ شَرِيْكَ لَهُ، لَهُ الْمُلْكُ وَ لَهُ الْحَمْدُ وَ هُوَ عَلَى كُلِّ شَيْءٍ قَدِيْر، وَ سُبْحَانَ اللهِ وَ الْحَمْدُ للهِ وَ لاَ إِلَهَ إِلاَّ اللهُ وَ لاَ حَوْلَ وَ لاَ قُوَّةَ إِلاَّ بِاللهِ»} $$

«None has the right to be worshipped except Al-laah, alone, without any partner, to Him belong sovereignty and praise and He is over all things wholly capable. And how perfect Allaah is, and all praise is for Allaah, and none has the right to be worshipped except Allaah, Allaah is the greatest and there is no power nor might except with Al-laah»

...and facing the *qiblah*, he [should] raise his hands in supplication, starting off by praising Allaah and sending salutations upon the Prophet (*sal-Allaahu 'alayhi wa sallam*).

And all of 'Arafah is a standing place [for the pilgrim]; And when the sun sets, it is legislated for the pilgrims to depart to Muzdalifah in peace and tranquility, whilst increasing in reciting the *talbiyah*.

So when they reach Muzdalifah, they are to perform the *Maghrib* and *'Ishaa* prayers after once *adhaan* and two *iqaamahs*; 3 *rak'ahs* are to be performed for *Maghrib* and 2 *rak'ahs* for the *'Ishaa* [prayers].

Shaykh Ibn Baaz

Chapter Eleven

Spending the night in Muzdalifah

1. All of Muzdalifah is a resting place

Question: During *hajj* this year, after departing from 'Arafah, I went to Muzdalifah and spent the night there but did not go to *al-Mash'ar al-Haraam* [which is now the site of the *masjid* in Muzdalifah]; So have I sinned [in not going to *al-Mash'ar al-Haraam*]?[1]

Response: You have not sinned; So long as you spent the night in any part of Muzdalifah, there is no harm if you did not go to *al-Mash'ar al-Haraam*. The Prophet (*sal-Allaahu 'alayhe wa sallam*) stopped by at *al-Mash'ar al-Haraam* and said:

«*I have stopped by here, however, all of Muzdalifah is a resting place*»[2]

...so it is sufficient to stop over at any place in Muzdalifah and spend the night there.

---

1 Fataawa al-Hajj wal-'Umrah waz-Ziyaarah - Pages 101-102.

2 al-Mu'jam al-Kabeer lit-Tabaraanee/11001 and 12199.

And that which is apparent from the statement of the Prophet (*sal-Allaa-hu 'alayhe wa sallam*) is that it is not befitting for a person to exert and inconvenience himself for the sake of getting to *al-Mash'ar al-Haraam*, rather he should stop over at any place [within Muzdalifah]. Then in the morning he should offer the *Fajr* prayer and supplicate to Allaah (*'Azza wa Jall*) and then depart for Minaa.

Shaykh Muhammad ibn 'Uthaymeen

2. Left Muzdalifah at midnight to stone Jamarah al-'Aqabah

Question: We left Muzdalifah with our children at 11:40pm, and then stoned the *jamarah* [*al-'aqabah*] pillar at 11:50pm, and afterwards pro-ceeded to Makkah; So what is the ruling?[3]

Response: You are not liable for any penalty, because the time at which you left Muzdalifah corresponded to the middle of the night; However, if you delayed [your departure] until the moon had set, then that would have been better and more careful.

May Allaah grant everyone success in that which is His Pleasure and may He accept [the righteous actions] from us and you and all the Muslims.

Shaykh 'Abdul-'Azeez ibn Baaz

3. Neglecting to spend the night in Muzdalifah

Question: What is the ruling regarding the pilgrim who neglected to spend the night in Muzdalifah [after departing from 'Arafah on 9th *Dhul-*

---

3 Fataawa al-Hajj wal-'Umrah waz-Ziyaarah - Page 102.

Hijjah]?[4]

Response: All pilgrims are required to spend the night in Muzdalifah, whilst the weak amongst them are legally permitted to depart during the last part of the night. And whoever intentionally neglects [to spend the night in Muzdalifah] has sinned, and as a result - according to the majority of the people of knowledge, is required to pay a penalty. As for he who unknowingly neglected to do so, then there is no sin upon him, instead, he is only required to pay a penalty.

However, just as with all other obligations, this obligation is waived for the frail and weak; But whoever catches the *Fajr* prayer at its initial time, and remains until after the prayer, and engages in the remembrance of Allaah, and then departs Muzdalifah for Minaa, then this is sufficient for him.

Shaykh Muhammad ibn 'Uthaymeen

4. Proceeded to Namirah assuming it to be Muzdalifah

Question: A pilgrim proceeded to *Namirah* assuming it to be Muzdalifah, so what is the ruling regarding his *hajj*?[5]

Response: Whoever proceeded to *Namirah* assuming it to be Muzdalifah, then he is liable for a penalty, because he fell short [of what was expected of him by] not having asked [about this at the time, i.e; exactly where Muzdalifah was]; However, their *hajj* is [still] valid.

Shaykh Muhammad ibn 'Uthaymeen

---

4   Fataawa al-Hajj wal-'Umrah waz-Ziyaarah - Page 99.

5   Fataawa al-Hajj wal-'Umrah waz-Ziyaarah - Page 101;
    I'laam al-Mu'aasireen bi-Fataawa Ibn 'Uthaymeen - Page 144.

5. Spending only the first half of the night in Muzdalifah

Question: What is the ruling regarding spending the night in Muzdalifah before the first half [of the night]?[6]

Response: It is obligatory upon the pilgrim to spend the entire night [in Muzdalifah] through till [the time of] *Fajr*, except for the one who has a legal excuse such as illness or the like. So, it is permissible for him or whoever has undertaken the responsibility for him to depart to Minaa after half the night has passed in accordance with the [example of the] Prophet (*Sal-Allaahu 'alayhe wa sallam*) who spent the night there until [the time of] *Fajr*, and granted those with a legal excuse to depart from Muzdalifah to Minaa after half the night [had passed].

Shaykh 'Abdul-'Azeez ibn Baaz

6. Spending the night in Muzdalifah

Question: What is the ruling regarding spending the night in Muzdalifah? [And] what is the duration of the stay there - when does it begin and when does the pilgrim depart from there?[7]

Response: According to the correct opinion [in this matter], spending the night in Muzdalifah is obligatory; Some of the people of knowledge have said it is a pillar [of *hajj*], whilst others [from amongst them] have said it is recommended. And that which is correct from the opinions of the people of knowledge is that it is certainly obligatory. Whoever does not do so, then he is required to offer a sacrifice [by slaughtering

---

6 Fataawa al-Hajj wal-'Umrah waz-Ziyaarah, Page 98.

7 Fataawa al-Hajj wal-'Umrah waz-Ziyaarah - Page 98.

a sheep and distributing its meat to the poor and needy of the people of Makkah].

And it is from the *Sunnah* not to depart from there until after the *Fajr* prayer - after it has brightened up; So he prays the *Fajr* prayer there, and once it brightens up, he heads for Minaa pronouncing the *talbiyah*. And it is from the *Sunnah* to engage in the remembrance of Allaah after the prayer and to supplicate and when it brightens up, to head for Minaa pronouncing the *talbiyah*.

And the Prophet (*sal-Allaahu 'alayhe wa sallam*) sanctioned for the debilitated amongst the men and the women, as well as the elderly to depart from Muzdalifah during the second half of the night. As for the others, then it is from the *Sunnah* that they remain [in Muzdalifah] until they pray the *Fajr* prayer, engage in much remembrance of Allaah after the prayer, and then depart before sunrise. It is [also] from the *Sunnah*, whilst they are in Muzdalifah, to raise their hands in supplication facing the *qiblah*, just as they did in 'Arafah; And all of Muzdalifah is a resting place.

Shaykh 'Abdul-'Azeez ibn Baaz

7. Unable to find a place to rest in Muzdalifah during night

Question: What is the ruling regarding the pilgrim who was unable to find a place [to rest] in Muzdalifah during the night before 'Eed [after having departed from 'Arafah]?[8]

Response: Whoever is unable to find a place [to rest] in Muzdalifah, then

---

8 Fataawa al-Hajj wal-'Umrah waz-Ziyaarah - Page 101.

that which is apparent is he is not liable for any penalty, because all obligatory acts are waived if one is [legally classified as being] unable to perform them.

Shaykh Muhammad ibn 'Uthaymeen

8. Unable to spend the night in Muzdalifah

Question: Whoever does not spend the night in Muzdalifah because he was unable to do so for whatever reason - such as having got lost or other than that - is he required to atone [for this]? May Allaah reward you with good.[9]

Response: Yes, that which is apparent is that he is required to atone [for this] according to the principles [laid down by the] people of knowledge, however there is no sin upon him [for having done so]. That is because the one who abstained from an obligation is excused [if he had a legally acceptable reason for doing so], therefore there is no sin upon him, instead he is required to compensate [for this] - that being to atone.

If, however, he did so intentionally, then upon him is the sin as well as the atonement; That which is apparent is that he is required to atone according to the principles [laid down by the] people of knowledge; Yes - if a person was coercively prevented from spending the night in Muzdalifah, then he is not liable for any penalty because this was done against his will.

Shaykh Muhammad ibn 'Uthaymeen

---

9 ad-Durrar an-Naadhirah fil-Fataawa al-Mu'aasirah - Page 410;
   ad-Da'wah 1494 - Muharram 1416 AH.

Chapter Twelve

Stoning the Jamaraat Pillars

1. A stone missed the pillar and fell into the pit

Question: What is required of the one who [accidentally] threw one of the [required seven] stones into the pit of the *Jamarah al-Kubraa* pillar due to the extreme overcrowding which exhausted him?[1]

Response: If it is possible, he should throw a [single] stone to compensate for the [earlier] missed stone, otherwise what he has already thrown is sufficient for him and he is not liable for any sacrificial penalty nor to feed the poor.

And with Allaah lies all success and may Allaah send prayers and salutations upon our Prophet (*sal-Allaahu 'alayhe wa sallam*) and his family and his Companions.

The Permanent Committee for Islaamic Research and Verdicts

---

1 Fataawa al-Hajj wal-'Umrah waz-Ziyaarah - Page 114.

2. Appointing someone else to do the stoning

Question: My mother and two sisters appointed me to throw the stones at the *jamaraat* pillars on their behalf because they feared the severe overcrowding, so is this correct?[2]

Response: It is acceptable to appoint someone on their behalf if they are frail and weak to do the stoning themselves due to the severe overcrowding, or they are ill or for any other legislated reason.

Shaykh 'Abdul-'Azeez ibn Baaz

3. Being in the state of purity and cleanliness when stoning

Question: Is it a requirement to be in a state of purity [*wudhoo*] when stoning the *jamaraat* [pillars]?[3]

Response: No. It is not a requirement to be in a state of purity [*wudhoo*] for any of the rights of the *hajj*, except for the *tawaaf* around the *Ka'bah*, since it is not permissible for the menstruating woman to perform *tawaaf* around the *Ka'bah* due to the saying of the Prophet (*sal-Allaahu 'alayhe wa sallam*) to 'Aa.ishah (*radhi-yAllaahu 'anhaa*):

«Do whatever the hajj pilgrim does apart from performing tawaaf around the House (Ka'bah)»[4]

Shaykh Muhammad ibn 'Uthaymeen

---

2 Fataawa al-Hajj wal-'Umrah waz-Ziyaarah - Page 118.

3 Fataawa al-Hajj wal-'Umrah - Page 53.

4 Saheeh Muslim/120, Sunan ad-Daarimee/1888, Saheeh Ibn Hibbaan/3835, Mustakhraj Abee 'Awaanah/3178.

4. Delaying stoning of Pillars due to ill health or crowding

Question: If the pilgrim delays the stoning of the *jamaraat* pillars until the days of *tashreeq*[5] due to an illness or [experiencing hardship due to] old age, or fear of overcrowding, is he then required to stone the *jamarah al-'aqabah* [pillar] and the other *jamaraat* [pillars] once [seven times each], or is he required to stone [each pillar] individually for each day - meaning that he stones [each pillar] for the first day, then he begins [stoning each pillar] again for the second day and like this [he proceeds] for the third day - even if therein is hardship?[6]

Response: He is first required to stone the *jamarah al-'aqabah*; He is then required to stone [all three of] the *jamaraat* [pillars] for the 11th day [of *Dhul-Hijjah*], then [to stone] the *jamaraat* [pillars] for the 12th day and then the 13th day - so long as he has not decided to [legally] shorten the *hajj* [by departing Minaa before sunset on the 12th day]; And it is from the *Sunnah* to [stone each of the pillars] on it's respective day in accordance with [one's] ability.

And with Allaah lies all success and may Allaah send prayers and salutations upon our Prophet (*sal-Allaahu 'alayhe wa sallam*) and his family and his Companions.

The Permanent Committee for Islaamic Research and Verdicts

5. Delaying the stoning until the night

Question: Is it permissible for the pilgrim who has no excuse to stone

---

5 The 11th, 12th and 13th days of Dhul-Hijjah.

6 Fataawa al-Hajj wal-'Umrah waz-Ziyaarah - Page 118.

the three *jamaraat* [pillars] during the night of the days of *tashreeq*[7] to do so? And is it permissible for those [from the pilgrims] who departed from Muzdalifah after midnight with the women and the debilitated to stone the *jamarah al-'aqabah* or not?[8]

Response: According to the correct opinion [in this matter], it is permissible to stone [the pillars] after sunset. However, the *Sunnah* is to stone [the pillars] after *zawaal* [which is when the sun above is at its highest point casting no shadow] and before sunset - this is best if it is possible. And if it is not possible, then according to the correct opinion [in this matter] he can stone [the pillars] after sunset.

And whoever from amongst the *mahrams*, the drivers and other than them departed Muzdalifah with the women and the debilitated, then their ruling is [the same as the ruling of the women and the debilitated] that it is permissible for them to stone [the pillars] during the last part of the night with the women.

Shaykh 'Abdul-'Azeez ibn Baaz

6. Description of the stones to be used for stoning

Question: From where are the stones to be gathered for stoning the *jamaraat* [pillars]; What is their description and what is the ruling regarding washing them?[9]

Response: The stones are to be gathered from Minaa, and if they are

---

7 The 11th, 12th and 13th days of Dhul-Hijjah.

8 Fataawa al-Hajj wal-'Umrah waz-Ziyaarah - Page 113.

9 Fataawa al-Hajj wal-'Umrah waz-Ziyaarah - Page 107.

picked up from Muzdalifah the night before the day of *'Eed*, then there is no harm in that; They are to be seven [in number] for [stoning the *jamarah al-'aqabah* pillar on] the day of *'Eed*, and it has not been legislated that they be washed, rather they are to be picked up in Minaa or Muzdalifah or even from anywhere else within the *Haram* precinct - and they are to be used for stoning [the pillars].

As for [the stones for] the days of *tashreeq*[10], they are to be gathered from Minaa; 21 stones are required for each day, amounting to 42 stones for the 11th and 12th days if [the pilgrim intends to] legally shorten his *hajj* [after the 12th day]; And if he does not intend to legally shorten his *hajj*, then he will require 63 stones.

[And] the stones are to be pelting stones resembling the average size of sheep or goat droppings - a little larger than the size of chick peas and a little smaller than hazelnuts, just as the jurists have referred to them as pelting stones as has been mentioned [previously] - and that they are a little smaller than sheep or goat droppings.

Shaykh 'Abdul-'Azeez ibn Baaz

7. Doubtful about how many stones thrown

Question: What is the ruling regarding the one who stones [the pillars] more than [the required] seven stones out of fear that some of them did not fall into the pit [after striking the pillars]?[11]

Response: There is no harm [in that]; If he has any doubt as to whether

---

10 The 11th, 12th and 13th days of Dhul-Hijjah.

11 Fataawa al-Hajj wal-'Umrah - Page 51.

he threw seven stones or less, he can continue to stone [the pillar(s)] until he feels sure that he has thrown seven stones and they have [all] fallen into the pit. Rather, that is obligatory upon him [to do], unless he is of an acute doubtful disposition or if he suddenly feels doubtful once he has completed the stoning - in which case he should not pay any attention to this doubt.

[Importantly], he must take care that he is close to the pit so that he does not make any mistakes when stoning [the pillars].

Shaykh Muhammad ibn 'Uthaymeen

8. Doubtful about the stones not having fallen into the pit

Question: What is the ruling regarding the one who becomes doubtful that some of the [pelting] stones did not fall into the pit [surrounding the pillars]?[12]

Response: Whoever has any doubt, then he is required to repeat the stoning [according to the number of [pelting] stones he feels did not fall into the pit]; [So] he collects the [pelting] stones from the ground in Minaa and completes [what remains of] the stoning.

Shaykh 'Abdul-'Azeez ibn Baaz

9. Legally shortening the Hajj

Question: When the *hajj* pilgrim decides to [legally] shorten his *hajj* [by stoning the *jamaraat* pillars on the 11th and 12th days of *Dhul-Hijjah*

---

12 Fataawa al-Hajj wal-'Umrah waz-Ziyaarah - Page 113.

and abstaining on the 13th day], but is unable to depart from Minaa before sunest after having [earlier] stoned the *jamaraat* pillars [before sunest], is he then required to remain in Minaa for the 13th day [of *Dhul-Hijjah*] or is he permitted to leave [Minaa even] after sunset?[13]

Response: If the *hajj* pilgrim did not leave Minaa before sunset [having stoned the *jamaraat* pillars on the 12th day of *Dhul-Hijjah*], then he is required to remain the night in Minaa. He is then required to stone all three *jamaraat* pillars after the *zawaal* [which is when the sun above is at its highest point casting no shadow] on the 13th day of *Dhul-Hijjah*. This is because it is a condition for the one who decides to [legally] shorten his *hajj* [by stoning the *jamaraat* pillars on the 11th and 12th days of *Dhul-Hijjah* and abstaining on the 13th day] - that he depart from Minaa before sunset on the 12th day [of *Dhul-Hijjah*].

Shaykh Saalih ibn Fowzaan

10. Picking stones from within the pit

Question: When I performed *hajj*, during the stoning [of the pillars], one of my stones fell out of my hands due to overcrowding and jostling. So all I was able to do [in that situation] was pick a used stone from the pit. I was unaware it was not permissible to use used stones, so what [penalty] am I liable for? I request [legal] clarity.[14]

Response: Picking stones for stoning the *jamaraat* [pillars] from within

---

13 ad-Durar an-Naadhirah fil-Fataawa al-Mu'aasirah - Page 418;
    ad-Da'wah 1503 - Rabee' al-Awwal 1416AH.

14 Fataawa lil-Hujjaaj wal-Mu'tamireen - Question 191, Page 146-147;
    Fataawa al-Lajnah ad-Daa.imah - Volume 11, Page 278.

the pit and then using them for stoning is not permissible because they have been used. However, so long as that which was picked was only a single stone, we hope Allaah overlooks that which has come to pass from you.

And with Allaah lies all success and may Allaah send prayers and salutations upon our Prophet (*sal-Allaahu 'alayhe wa sallam*) and his family and his Companions.

The Permanent Committee for Islaamic Research and Verdicts

11. Specific supplication after stoning the Jamaraat pillars

Question: Is there any specific supplication [to be made after stoning the pillars]?[15]

Response: From that which I am aware of, there is no specific [legislated] supplication [to be made].

Shaykh Muhammad ibn 'Uthaymeen

12. Stoned pillars before Zawaal

Question: What is required of the one who stoned the *jamaraat* [pillars] during *dhuhaa* (the period between after sunrise and before *zawaal* [which is when the sun above is at its highest point casting no shadow]) on the 11th day [of *Dhul-Hijjah*], and then discovered that the time for

---

15 Fataawa al-Hajj wal-'Umrah - Page 53.

stoning [the *jamaraat* pillars] is actually after *Zhuhr*[16]?[17]

Response: Whoever stones the *jamaraat* [pillars] on the 11th day [of *Dhul-Hijjah*] during the period between after sunrise and before *zawaal*, then he is required to repeat the stoning after midday on that day. And if he did not discover his error until the 12th day or the 13th day [of *Dhul-Hijjah*] - then he is required to stone [the pillars] after *zawaal* on the 12th day or the 13th day after *zawaal* - before he stones [the pillars] for that particular day; And if he did not discover [his error] until after sunset on the 13th day [of *Dhul-Hijjah*] and he did not stone [the pillars], then he is required to make an expiation by slaughtering [a sheep] in the *Haram* [area] and with it feed the poor and needy.

And with Allaah lies all success and may Allaah send prayers and salutations upon our Prophet (*sal-Allaahu 'alayhe wa sallam*) and his family and his Companions.

The Permanent Committee for Islaamic Research and Verdicts

13. Stoned the pillars in the opposite direction

Question: A relative of mine performed the obligatory [first] *hajj* in 1406AH. On the first day of stoning the *jamaraat* [pillars], instead of stoning the pillars beginning with the smallest one, then the middle and then the largest one, he did so in the opposite manner [beginning with the largest and so on]. He became aware of this mistake on the second day whereby he corrected himself and did the stoning in the prescribed manner on the second and third days, without rectifying the mistake

---

16 i.e. after zawaal.

17 Fataawa al-Hajj wal-'Umrah waz-Ziyaarah - Page 116.

of the first day or compensating for it. Thereafter he completed all the rituals [of *hajj*] and returned to his country. He has now written asking about what is required of him regarding this error, since everyone he has asked differs in opinion.[18]

Response: He is required to pay a penalty by sacrificing a seventh part of a camel or a cow, or one goat or sheep which must be a male sheep or a female goat - to be sacrificed in Makkah and distributed to the poor and needy there. This is because he was aware of the ruling [of his error] on the second day and did not repeat the stoning [to compensate for this error] as is legislated. It has been confirmed on the authority of Ibn 'Abbaas (*radhi-yAllaahu 'anhumaa*) who said:

> «*Whoever misses an obligatory rite [from the rites of the hajj or the 'umrah] then he is required to pay a penalty*»[19]

...and this [statement] assumes the ruling of being attributed to the Prophet (*sal-Allaahu 'alayhe wa sallam*) because Ibn 'Abbaas (*radhi-yAllaahu 'anhumaa*) did not make it in a manner that he was offering an opinion; There is also no known conflicting viewpoint from [any of] the [other] Companions (*radhi-yAllaahu 'anhum*).

And with Allaah lies all success.

Shaykh 'Abdul-'Azeez ibn Baaz

---

18 Fataawa al-Hajj wal-'Umrah waz-Ziyaarah - Page 116.

19 Muwatta Maalik/240, Musnad Ibnul-Ja'd/1749, Sunan ad-Daaraqutnee/2534.

14. Stoning before midday due to extreme circumstances

Question: What is the ruling regarding the one who spent two days after the 'Eed[20] [in Minaa] and [then] spent the night of the 12th day [in Minaa]; Due to extreme circumstances, is it permissible for him to stone [the pillars] after sunrise, or [must he only do so] after midday?[21]

Response: Whoever remained in Minaa until nightfall (sunset) on the 12th day, then he is required to spend the night and then stone [the pillars the following day] after midday. It is not permissible for him to stone [the pillars] before midday - as [he had done] in the previous two days; He is not allowed to stone [the pillars] until after midday because the Messenger (sal-Allaahu 'alayhe wa sallam) remained in Minaa until the 13th day [of Dhul-Hijjah] and did not stone [the pillars] until after midday [as] he (sal-Allaahu 'alayhe wa sallam) said:

«Take from me your rites [of Hajj]»[22]

Shaykh 'Abdul-'Azeez ibn Baaz

15. Stoning each pillar using more than seven stones

Question: If a pilgrim exceeds the required number of stones used - for example if he was to stone [each of the pillars] using ten or more [stones], would he be liable for any penalty?[23]

---

20 The 11th and 12th days of Dhul-Hijjah.

21 Fataawa al-Hajj wal-'Umrah waz-Ziyaarah - Page 117.

22 as-Sunan al-Kubraa lil-Bayhaqee/9524.

23 Fataawa lil-Hujjaaj wal-Mu'tamireen - Question 188, Pages 144-145.

Response: Whoever exceeds the use of [the required number of] seven stones during the stoning [of each pillar], then this will suffice; However, he has done wrong in exceeding.

And with Allaah lies all success and may Allaah send prayers and salutations upon our Prophet (*sal-Allaahu 'alayhe wa sallam*) and his family and his Companions.

The Permanent Committee for Islaamic Research and Verdicts

16. Stoned 11th day & performed Tawaaf before travelling

Question: What is the ruling concerning one who stones [the *jama-raat* pillars] on the 11th day [of *Dhul-Hijjah*], then performs *tawaaf al-wadaa'* around the House (*Ka'bah*) before travelling?[24]

Response: If he stones [the *jamaraat* pillars] on the 11th day [of Dhul-Hijjah], then performs *tawaaf al-wadaa'* around the House (*Ka'bah*) and then travels, he has neglected two obligations - and they are the stoning of the *jamaraat* [pillars] on the 12th day [of *Dhul-Hijjah*] and remaining in Minaa the night prior to the 12th day [of *Dhul-Hijjah*]. So, he is therefore required to make two *fidyah*'s (ransoms) [as compensation] according to the opinion of many of the people of knowledge; So he must slaughter them in Makkah and distribute [the meat] there.

Shaykh Muhammad ibn 'Uthaymeen

---

24 Fataawa al-Hajj wal-'Umrah waz-Ziyaarah - Page 117.

17. Stoning the pillars in the correct order

Question: A man stoned the *jamaraat* [pillars], beginning with *al-ku-braa* before *as-sughraa*. So what is he required to do?[25]

Response: He is required to repeat [the stoning for] *al-wustaa* and then the final one - *al-kubraa*; In this way he will have stoned them after *as-sughraa* [which he stoned earlier], and with that he will then have stoned *as-sughraa*, then *al-wustaa*, and thereafter *al-kubraa* [in the required order].

Shaykh 'Abdul-'Azeez ibn Baaz

18. Supplicating after stoning the Jamaraat pillars

Question: Are we required to make any supplication when stoning the *jamaraat* [pillars]?[26]

Response: Yes, we have [previously] mentioned that after stoning the first *jamarah* [pillar], turn to face the *Ka'bah* and raise your hands in supplication. And you stand there making a lengthy supplication; Like-wise, you do so after stoning the *jamarah al-wustaa* [pillar]. As for after stoning the *jamarah al-'aqabah* [pillar], then you must not stand [and supplicate].

Shaykh Muhammad ibn 'Uthaymeen

---

25   Fataawa lil-Hujjaaj wal-Mu'tamireen - Question 187, Page 144.

26   Fataawa al-Hajj wal-'Umrah - Page 53.

19. Using the stones outside the pit for stoning

Question: Is it permissible for the pilgrim to stone [the pillars] using the [pelting] stones he finds around (outside) the pit [of the *jamaraat* pillars]?[27]

Response: That is permissible for him to do because it is apparent [by the fact they are found outside the pit that] they have not struck the *jamaraat* pillars; As for those stones which are within the pit, then they are not to be used whatsoever [as they have already struck the *jamaraat* pillars - and are now considered 'used'].

Shaykh 'Abdul-'Azeez ibn Baaz

20. Washing the stones picked for stoning the pillars

Question: What is the ruling regarding washing the stones [picked] for stoning the pillars?[28]

Response: They are not to be washed; Rather, if a person washed them thinking this to be a rewarding act [of worship] and one that will bring him closer to Allaah then this is an innovation because the Prophet (*sal-Allaahu 'alayhe wa sallam*) did not [instruct us to] do this.

Shaykh Muhammad ibn 'Uthaymeen

---

27 Fataawa al-Hajj wal-'Umrah waz-Ziyaarah - Page 108.

28 I'laam al-Mu'aasireen bi-Fataawa Ibn 'Uthaymeen - Page 147.

Chapter Thirteen

The Sacrifice

1. Carrying out the sacrifice and then leaving it

Question: What is the ruling regarding the one who slaughters his sacrifice and then leaves it; Will he be rewarded [for having performed the sacrifice] or not?[1]

Response: The one who slaughters his sacrifice is required to make sure it reaches those who are genuinely deserving [of it - from amongst the poor and destitute]. It is not permissible to slaughter [the sacrifice] and then leave it. And if he were to take a little from it and eat it, and [then] give [the remainder] in charity [to the poor and destitute], then this is sufficient.

Shaykh Muhammad ibn 'Uthaymeen

13

---

1 Fataawa al-Hajj wal-'Umrah waz-Ziyaarah - Page 124.

2. Offering a sacrifice on behalf of the deceased

Question: Is it from the *Sunnah* of [slaughtering] the sacrifice to do so on behalf of the father, particularly if he has died?[2]

Response: It is not from the *Sunnah* that a person slaughters the sacrifice specifically on behalf of the deceased. [Rather], it is from the *Sunnah* for a person to slaughter the sacrifice on behalf of the whole family; And if he made the intention that it be on behalf of the living and the deceased of the family, then there is no harm in this as the blessings of Allaah are abundant.

As for specifically doing so on behalf of the deceased and not the living, then this is not from the *Sunnah*, [as] it has not been [authentically] established that the Prophet (*sal-Allaahu 'alayhe wa sallam*) ever slaughtered the sacrifice specifically for [any of] the dead.

Shaykh Muhammad ibn 'Uthaymeen

3. Regarding 'Foot and Mouth' disease

It is permissible for Muslims living in Europe not to sacrifice animals during this *'Eed al-Adhaa* festival because of the 'foot-and-mouth' disease[3]. If Muslims in Europe find themselves in a situation where they are prevented from sacrificing a [sacrificial] animal - after what has been

---

2 al-Fataawa al-Muhimmah - Page 748;
   Liqaa.aat al-Baab al-Maftooh - No.571.

3 An infectious and sometimes fatal viral disease that affects cloven-hoofed animals, including domestic and wild bovids, i.e. bison, African buffalo, water buffalo, antelopes, gazelles, sheep, goats, muskoxen, and domestic cattle.

reported about the state of the animal, they must abide by the rules. The sacrifice of a [sacrificial] animal is not an obligation for Muslims, rather it is a *Sunnah*. Those who have the means to sacrifice a [sacrificial] animal can do so. For those who do not, it is not obligatory.[4]

Shaykh 'Abdul-'Azeez Aal ash-Shaykh

4. Residents of Makkah not required to sacrifice

<u>Question</u>: Are the residents of Makkah intending to perform *hajj* required to make a sacrificial offering? And which of the two are they permitted to undertake - the *tamattu'* or the *qiraan hajj*? We request clarification of this matter inclusive of the evidence.[5]

<u>Response</u>: The residents of Makkah and other than them are permitted to undertake the *tamattu'* as well as the *qiraan hajj*, however the residents of Makkah [specifically] are not required to make a sacrificial offering. Rather, the sacrificial offering is required of others who have travelled from outside Makkah intending [to perform] the *tamattu'* or the *qiraan hajj*. This is based upon the saying of Allaah (*Subhaanahu wa Ta'aala*):

$$فَمَن تَمَتَّعَ بِٱلْعُمْرَةِ إِلَى ٱلْحَجِّ$$

$$فَمَا ٱسْتَيْسَرَ مِنَ ٱلْهَدْيِ فَمَن لَّمْ يَجِدْ فَصِيَامُ ثَلَٰثَةِ أَيَّامٍ فِي ٱلْحَجِّ وَسَبْعَةٍ$$

$$إِذَا رَجَعْتُمْ تِلْكَ عَشَرَةٌ كَامِلَةٌ ذَٰلِكَ لِمَن لَّمْ يَكُنْ أَهْلُهُ حَاضِرِي$$

$$ٱلْمَسْجِدِ ٱلْحَرَامِ وَٱتَّقُوا ٱللَّهَ وَٱعْلَمُوا أَنَّ ٱللَّهَ شَدِيدُ ٱلْعِقَابِ$$

---

4 Announcement made by the Shaykh on Monday 5 March, 2001.

5 Fataawa al-Hajj wal-'Umrah waz-Ziyaarah - Pages 122-123.

...and whosoever performs the 'umrah in the months of hajj, before (performing) the hajj, he must slaughter a hady such as he can afford, but if he cannot afford it, he should observe saum (fasts) three days during the hajj and seven days after his return (to his home), making ten days in all. This is for him whose family is not present at al-Masjid al-Haraam (i.e. non-resident of Makkah). And fear Allaah much and know that Allaah is Severe in punishment.[6]

Shaykh 'Abdul-'Azeez ibn Baaz

5. Slaughtering the Sacrifice before the day of 'Eed

Question: What is the opinion of your eminence regarding the one who slaughtered the sacrifice of the *tamattu'* or the *qiraan* [*hajj*] before the day of *'Eed*, citing as their proof the statement of some of the *imaams* of the Islaamic schools of jurisprudence who permit that?[7]

Response: Whoever slaughtered the sacrifice of the *tamattu'* or *qiraan* [*hajj*] before the day of *'Eed* [due to] following those who hold this viewpoint, [then] he is not liable for any penalty; However, they need to be advised against doing so in the future.

Shaykh Muhammad ibn 'Uthaymeen

---

6 The Noble Qur.aan - Soorah al-Baqarah, Aayah 196.

7 Fataawa al-Hajj wal-'Umrah waz-Ziyaarah - Page 125.

6. Slaughtering the sacrifice outside Makkah

Question: Is it permissible to slaughter the sacrifice outside the holy land [of Makkah], particularly in the land of the pilgrim [for example]?[8]

Response: The [legislated] place for the sacrifice [to be carried out] is within the Makkan sanctuary; So it is obligatory to carry out all the sacrifices for the *tamattu'* [*hajj*] and the *qiraan* [*hajj*] within this sanctuary. It is not permissible to [carry out the] slaughter in the land of the pilgrim outside Makkah, rather, if the sacrificial animal is wounded prior to reaching Makkah, then [in this case] it can be slaughtered wherever it has [become wounded] - and this will suffice [the pilgrim for his *hajj*]. Likewise, regarding the one whose circumstances prevent him from completing the *hajj* - upon entering Makkah, he may slaughter his sacrificial animal where he is prevented [from completing the *hajj*].

And with Allaah lies all success and may Allaah send prayers and salutations upon our Prophet (*sal-Allaahu 'alayhe wa sallam*) and his family and his Companions.

The Permanent Committee for Islaamic Research and Verdicts

7. The merit in slaughtering the sacrifice earlier

Question: Is there any difference in the merit between slaughtering the sacrifice on the first, second or third days?[9]

---

8 Fataawa lil-Hujjaaj wal-Mu'tamireen - Question 200, Page 153-154;
   Fataawa al-Lajnah ad-Daa.imah - Volume 11, Page 38.

9 Fataawa lil-Hujjaaj wal-Mu'tamireen - Question 201, Page 154;
   Majmoo' Fataawa Ibn Baaz - Volume 7, Page 262.

Response: Yes. The first day is better, and the second day is better than the third, and the third [day] is better than the fourth; So, the earlier [it is carried out], the better.

Shaykh 'Abdul-'Azeez ibn Baaz

8. The penalty of the ignorant and the forgetful one

Question: Regarding the one who is ignorant about a ruling, or the one who has forgetfully missed an obligatory rite from the rites of *hajj*, such as spending the night [in Minaa or Muzdalifah] or stoning [the *jamaraat* pillars] or shaving the head - is the penalty [for doing so] waived or is it still applicable? Likewise, in the situation where someone has committed a prohibited act [not permissible] whilst in the state of *ihraam*?[10]

Response: Regarding the ignorant and the one who forgetfully commits a prohibited act [not permissible] whilst in the state of *ihraam*, [then the penalty is] waived. [However] it is not waived for the one who missed an obligatory rite from the rites of the *hajj* or the *'umrah* - whether he did so out of ignorance or forgetfulness. This is based upon the statement of Ibn 'Abbaas (*radhi-yAllaahu 'anhumaa*) who said:

«Whoever misses an obligatory rite [from the rites of the hajj or the 'umrah] then he is required to pay a penalty»[11]

And likewise, the *hadeeth* about the owner of the long coat which was scented with perfume whilst he was in the state of [*ihraam*] performing

---

10 Fataawa al-Hajj wal-'Umrah waz-Ziyaarah - Page 119.

11 Muwatta Maalik/240, Musnad Ibnul-Ja'd/1749, Sunan ad-Daaraqutnee/2534.

'umrah.

And with Allaah lies all success and may Allaah send prayers and salutations upon our Prophet (sal-Allaahu 'alayhe wa sallam) and his family and his Companions.

The Permanent Committee for Islaamic Research and Verdicts

9. The sacrifice of 'Eed al-Adh.haa

Question: What is the correct opinion regarding the sacrifice (of 'Eed al-Adh.haa)?[12]

Response: That which is apparent to me is the sacrifice is not obligatory. However, it is a highly recommended Sunnah and is [therefore] disliked for one who is able [to offer it] to abstain from doing so.

Shaykh Muhammad ibn 'Uthaymeen

13

---

12 al-Fataawa al-Muhimmah - Page 743;
    Liqaa.aat al-Baab al-Maftooh - No.160.

Chapter Fourteen

Mistakes and Innovations

1. Entering al-Masjid al-Haraam through a particular door

<u>Question</u>: What are the mistakes some pilgrims commit when entering *al-Masjid al-Haraam*?[1]

<u>Response</u>: From amongst the mistakes that some pilgrims fall into when entering *al-Masjid al-Haraam* are - firstly: That some people think it is imperative, for performing *hajj* or *'umrah*, to enter through a particular door of *al-Masjid al-Haraam*. So, for example, some people deem it necessary for those performing *'umrah* to enter via the door which is called 'The *'Umrah* Door'[2], or that this is something that should be done and that it is legislated. Others see that it is imperative to enter via 'The Door of Peace'[3] and that entering through any other door is a sin or disliked - whilst there is no evidence to confirm this. So, those perform-

---

1 al-Bid'u wal-Muhdathaat wa maa laa Asla lahu - Page 384;
   Fiqh al-'Ibaadaat - Page 344.

2 Baab al-'Umrah.

3 Baab as-Salaam.

ing *hajj* or *'umrah* may enter via any door they wish, and when doing so, to extend the right foot first [upon entry] and pronounce [the supplication] which is mentioned for entering all *masaajid*. So, they send salutations upon the Prophet (*sal-Allaahu 'alayhe wa sallam*) and say:

> **«O Allaah! Forgive me my sins and open Your Doors of Mercy to me»**[4]

Secondly: Some people innovate certain supplications upon entering *al-Masjid al-Haraam* and seeing the House (*Ka'bah*). They innovate supplications which have not been mentioned by the Prophet (*sal-Allaahu 'alayhe wa sallam*), and they supplicate to Allaah with them. This is an innovation. Any act of worship, whether it be by speech, action or firm belief which the Prophet (*sal-Allaahu 'alayhe wa sallam*) or his Companions did not practice - is considered an innovation and [deemed] an evil - something which the Messenger of Allaah has [sternly] warned against.

Shaykh Muhammad ibn 'Uthaymeen

2. Gifting the reward of doing the Tawaaf to someone

Question: A woman asks: When I was in Makkah al-Mukarramah, I received news that a relative of mine had died; So I performed *tawaaf* on her behalf - seven times around the *Ka'bah* - and made the intention for

14

---

4 Saheeh Muslim/68, Sunan Abee Daawood/465, Sunan an-Nasaa.ee/729, Sunan Ibn Maajah/772, Sunan ad-Daarimee/1434, Saheeh Ibn Khuzaymah/452, Saheeh Ibn Hibbaan/2047.

her [to receive the reward]. Is this permissible?[5]

Response: Yes, it is permissible for you to perform the *tawaaf* - seven times - and render the reward for whoever you wish from the Muslims; This is what is common from the *madh.hab* of *Imaam* Ahmad (*rahima-hullaah*); Any act of worship a Muslim performs and gifts its reward for a(nother) Muslim, dead or alive, then that will benefit him whether it be [a] wholly physical [act of worship] such as the *salaah* and the *tawaaf* or [a] wholly monetary [act of worship] such as *sadaqah*, or a combination of the two such as offering a sacrifice.

However, it is befitting to know that which is best for a person is to render noble acts [of worship] for himself and [instead] to restrict himself to supplicating for whoever he wishes from the Muslims; That is because this is the guidance given to us by the Prophet (*sal-Allaahu 'alayhe wa sallam*) in his statement:

> *«If someone dies his actions come to a halt, except for three: Recurring charity [he has made], or knowledge which he has benefited [others] with, or a righteous son who prays for him»*[6]

Shaykh Muhammad ibn 'Uthaymeen

---

5 ad-Durar an-Naadhirah fil-Fataawa al-Mu'aasirah - Page 453; Ibn 'Uthaymeen - ad-Da'wah 1587, Dhul-Hijjah 1417AH.

6 Saheeh Muslim/14, Sunan Abee Daawood/2880, Musnad Ahmad/8189, Sunan ad-Daarimee/578, Musnad Abee Ya'laa/6457, Saheeh Ibn Khuzaymah/2494, Saheeh Ibn Hibbaan/3016.

3. Gifting reward of performing Tawaaf to someone else

Question: What is the ruling regarding 'gifting' the reward of performing *tawaaf* to someone else, whereby some people approach others and say to them: 'Do seven for me!', meaning seven circuits, intending the reward for themselves. So is this permissible or not?[7]

Response: It is not permisisble to perform *tawaaf* around the *Ka'bah* for someone else. So no-one should perform *tawaaf* for other than themselves unless he is performing *hajj* or *'umrah* [on behalf of someone else]; So he does so in entirety [completing the] *hajj* or *'umrah* [and not just a part thereof].

And with Allaah lies all success and may Allaah send prayers and salutations upon our Prophet (*sal-Allaahu 'alayhe wa sallam*) and his family and his Companions.

The Permanent Committee for Islaamic Research and Verdicts

4. Holding on to the Kiswah of the Ka'bah

Question: What is the ruling regarding the one who holds on to the covering (*Kiswah*) of the *Ka'bah* and supplicates for a long while?[8]

Response: There is no evidence from the *Sunnah* [to confirm the permissibility of] the action of these people, [in which case] it is an innovation and [therefore] befitting, rather, obligatory that a student of knowl-

---

7 Fataawa al-Lajnah ad-Daa.imah lil-Buhooth al-'Ilmiyyah wal-Iftaa. - Volume 11, Page 236, Fatwa No.8433.

8 I'laam al-Mu'aasireen bi-Fataawa Ibn 'Uthaymeen - Page 152.

edge explains this to them. Additionally, this is not from the guidance of the Prophet (*sal-Allaahu 'alayhe wa sallam*).

As for holding on to the area between *al-Hajar al-Aswad* and the door, then there is evidence from the action of the Companions [to confirm its permissibility] so there is no harm in [doing] that. However, with the crowds and the pushing that is witnessed nowadays, it is not befitting for a person to do that which causes harm to himself or to others [especially] in a matter which is not [even] obligatory.

Shaykh Muhammad ibn 'Uthaymeen

5. Passing reward for Salaah, Qur.aan and Tawaaf to parents

Question: It has been said that supplicating for the parents during the obligatory prayers is not permissible, and nor is [intending] to pass over to them the reward for completing the *Qur.aan* or [performing] the *tawaaf*.[9]

Response: There is no harm in supplicating during the prayer either for oneself or for one's parents; Rather this is legislated. The Prophet (*sal-Allaahu 'alayhe wa sallam*) said:

«The closest a servant is to his Lord is when he is in sujood, so increase in making the supplication [during it]»[10]

---

9 al-Bid'u wal-Muhdathaat wa maa laa Asla lahu - Page 382;
   Majallah al-Buhooth al-Islaamiyyah - Volume 46, Page 198.

10 Saheeh Muslim/215, al-Mu'jam al-Kabeer lit-Tabaraanee/10014.

And he (*sal-Allaahu 'alayhe wa sallam*) said:

> «*As for the rukoo', then magnify the Lord [during it], and as for the sujood then strive in making the supplication [during it], for it is worthy of being responded to*»[11]

And [it is reported] in the two Saheehs' [of *Imaam* al-Bukhaaree and *Imaam* Muslim], on the authority of Ibn Mas'ood (*radhi-yallaahu 'anhu*), that when the Prophet (*sal-Allaahu 'alayhe wa sallam*) taught him the *tashahhud*, he said:

> «*...then choose a supplication which pleases you and supplicate [with it]*»

And in another narration:

> «*...then choose from that which you desire*»

What is implied here is before the *tasleem*, so if he supplicates in the *sujood* or at the end of the prayer for himself, his parents or the Muslims, there is no harm [in doing so] for what is mentioned of the generality of these *ahaadeeth* and other than them. As for passing the reward for reciting [the *Qur.aan*] or performing the *tawaaf* for one's parents or other than them from the Muslims, then this is an issue in which there is a difference of opinion amongst the scholars. That which is better, is to leave this since no evidence exists for its permissibility. Acts of worship have been legislated, so nothing is to be practised unless legislated by the *Sharee'ah*, because the Prophet (*sal-Allaahu 'alayhe wa sallam*)

14

---

11 Saheeh Muslim, Musannaf Ibn Abee Shaybah/2559, Saheeh Ibn Hibbaan/1896.

said:

«Anyone who introduces something into this matter of ours (i.e. Islaam), that which is not from it, will have it rejected»[12]

And in another narration:

«Anyone who does an act which is not in agreement with us, then he will have it rejected»[13]

And Allaah is the Guardian of all Success.

Shaykh 'Abdul-'Azeez ibn Baaz

6. Jogging between the two green lights

Question: You previously mentioned from amongst the mistakes [the pilgrims make during *sa'ee*] is that they abandon the brisk jog between the two green lights, which are [positioned] closer to *Safaa*.[14]

Response: Yes, the brisk jog is not mandatory; However, it is better to do so between the two green lights when proceeding from *Safaa* to *Mar-*

---

12 Saheeh al-Bukhaaree/2697, Saheeh Muslim/17, Sunan Abee Daawood/4606, Sunan Ibn Maajah/14, Musnad Ahmad/26033, Mustakhraj Abee 'Awaanah/6407, Saheeh Ibn Hibbaan/27, Sunan ad-Daaraqutnee/4534.

13 Saheeh al-Bukhaaree, Saheeh Muslim/18, Musnad Ahmad/25472, Mustakhraj Abee 'Awaanah/6409, Sunan ad-Daaraqutnee/4537, al-Ibaanah al-Kubraa libni Battah/ 147.

14 Fataawaa al-Hajj wal-'Umrah - Page 86.

wah and [also] on the return from *Marwah* to *Safaa*. That is because it has been legislated [for the men] during every lap when passing the two green lights.

Shaykh Muhammad ibn 'Uthaymeen

7. Kissing the Yemeni corner

Question: Is it permissible to kiss the Yemeni corner [of the *Ka'bah*]?[15]

Response: [The act of] kissing the Yemeni corner[16] has not been [authentically] confirmed from the Messenger of Allaah (*sal-Allaahu 'alayhe wa sallam*). [Therefore], any act of worship which has not been confirmed from the Messenger of Allaah (*sal-Allaahu 'alayhe wa sallam*) is an innovation and not something [by] which [one] draws near to Allaah. So, based upon this, it is not legislated for a person to kiss the Yemeni corner since this has not been [authentically] established from the Prophet (*sal-Allaahu 'alayhe wa sallam*). Rather, it has been mentioned in a weak *hadeeth* that cannot be used as proof.

Shaykh Muhammad ibn 'Uthaymeen

8. Making a long supplication behind Maqaam Ibraaheem

Question: What is the ruling regarding making a long supplication be-

14

---

15 al-Bid'u wal-Muhdathaat wa maa laa Asla lahu - Page 388;
    Fiqh al-'Ibaadaat - Page 348.

16 ar-Rukn al-Yamaanee.

hind *maqaam* Ibraaheem?[17]

Response: From the innovations that some people do when they stand behind *maqaam* Ibraaheem is that they make a long supplication which they call *'du'aa al-maqaam'*. There is no basis for this from the *Sunnah* of the Messenger (*sal-Allaahu 'alayhe wa sallam*); This is an innovation which is prohibited, [and beware that] every innovation is [a door to] misguidance. Along with this being an innovation, some people hold [small] books which contain this supplication and they begin supplicating in a loud voice and those behind them respond by saying *'aameen'*. This is an innovation, and with this there is [unnecessary] interference with [other] worshippers [in prayer] around *maqaam* Ibraaheem. From that which has preceded, interference with worshippers [in prayer and general worship] is prohibited.

Shaykh Muhammad ibn 'Uthaymeen;

9. Performing ablution before carrying out the sacrifice

Question: The *imaam* in our town leads the people in prayer. However, on the day of *'Eed al-Adh.haa*, after leading the people in prayer, he performs ablution in front of everyone before he carries out the sacrifice. So, is it permissible to eat the meat from his sacrifice?[18]

Response: It has not been [authentically] established that the Prophet

---

17 al-Bid'u wal-Muhdathaat wa maa laa Asla lahu - Page 399;
    Fiqh al-'Ibaadaat - Page 356.

18 Fataawa al-Lajnah ad-Daa.imah lil-Buhooth al-'Ilmiyyah wal-Iftaa. - Question 4 of
    Fatwa No.1275;
    al-Bid'u wal-Muhdathaat wa maa laa asla lahu - Page 208.

(*sal-Allaahu 'alayhe wa sallam*) performed the ablution after the *'Eed al-Adh.haa* prayer to perform the sacrifice, and this is also not known from the Pious Predecessors, nor from the generations about whom the Prophet (*sal-Allaahu 'alayhe wa sallam*) bore witness to their good. So, the one who performs ablution to carry out the sacrifice is ignorant and an innovator. This is authentically established from the Prophet (*sal-Allaahu 'alayhe wa sallam*), who said:

«Whoever introduces anything into this matter of ours (i.e. Islaam) that which is not from it, will have it rejected»[19]

However, if he performed the ablution specifically to perform the sacrifice, he is still rewarded, so long as he is a Muslim, and nothing is known about him which would render him a disbeliever; [Only] then is it permissible for him and others to eat the meat of the sacrifice.

And with Allaah lies all success and may Allaah send prayers and salutations upon our Prophet (*sal-Allaahu 'alayhe wa sallam*) and his family and his Companions.

The Permanent Committee for Islaamic Research and Verdicts

10. Making Tawaaf around the Prophet's chamber

Question: What is the ruling regarding making *tawaaf* around the Prophet's chamber?[20]

14

---

19 Saheeh al-Bukhaaree/2697 and Saheeh Muslim/1718.

20 al-Bid'u wal-Muhdathaat wa maa laa asla lahu - Page 403.

<u>Response</u>: Some vistors to the Prophet's *Masjid* perform *tawaaf* around the grave of the Prophet (*sal-Allaahu 'alayhe wa sallam*) and touch the caging of the chamber and its walls, and possibly kiss it and place their cheeks upon it. All of this is a detestable innovation! Certainly, making *tawaaf* around other than the *Kab'ah* is impermissible; Also, touching, kissing and placing the cheeks has been legislated for a specific place on the *Ka'bah* (between *al-Hajar al-Aswad* and the door of the *Ka'bah*). So, worshipping Allaah in this way, on the walls of the chamber, does not increase a person in anything except distancing himself from Allaah.

Shaykh Muhammad ibn 'Uthaymeen

11. Mistakes which occur during the Tawaaf

<u>Question</u>: There are some mistakes which occur whilst performing *tawaaf*; What are those mistakes?[21]

<u>Response</u>: Many pilgrims adhere to specific supplications whilst performing *tawaaf*. There are groups from amongst them that take [their supplications] from someone designated to read, and then they all repeat this as a group in chorus. This is a mistake from two points:

Firstly: This is adhering to a supplication which has not been legislated [for whilst performing *tawaaf*], since no specific supplication has been transmitted on the authority of the Prophet (*sal-Allaahu 'alayhe wa sallam*) whilst performing *tawaaf*;

Secondly: The group supplication in chorus is an innovation, which

---

21 al-Bid'u wal-Muhdathaat wa maa laa Asla lahu - Page 398;
     al-Fataawa Fadheelatush-Shaykh Saalih ibn Fowzaan al-Fowzaan - Volume 2, Page 30.

also interferes with the [concentration of] other pilgrims performing *tawaaf*. That which is legislated is for everyone to supplicate on their own without raising the voices.

Shaykh Saalih ibn Fowzaan

12. Prolonging stand at beginning of each Tawaaf circuit

Question: When at the line demarcating the starting point for the *tawaaf*, some of the pilgrims stand at length and [thereby] prohibit their [approaching Muslim] brothers [and sisters] from continuing with their *tawaaf*. So what is the ruling regarding standing at length and supplicating at this line?[22]

Response: Standing at this line is not supposed to be lengthy, rather, one should face *al-Hajar al-Aswad* and [raising the right hand] make a sign towards it saying '*Allaahu Akbar*' and then start walking [around the *Ka'bah*]. This is not a place to lengthen one's stand at, yet I see some people standing [there] and saying: 'I have made the intention for '*um-rah* (or *naafilah*) to perform *tawaaf* seven times for the Sake of Allaah' or that which is similar. This is a clear mistake in [the understanding of what] the intention [means]. And we have [previously] advised about this, that any verbal pronouncing of the intention in acts of worship is an innovation, [something] which has not been [authentically] reported from the Prophet (*sal-Allaahu 'alayhe wa sallam*) and nor any of his Companions (*radhi-yAllaahu 'anhum*).

So you are doing an act of worship for the Sake of Allaah (*Subhaanahau wa Ta'aala*), and He is well aware of your intention, so there is no need

---

22 Fataawa al-Hajj wal-'Umrah - Page 76.

to verbally pronounce the intention.

Shaykh Muhammad ibn 'Uthaymeen

13. Intention for Salaah, Wudhoo, Tawaaf and Sa'ee

Question: What is the ruling regarding pronouncing the intention for the *salaah*, *wudhoo*, *tawaaf* and *sa'ee*?[23]

Response: Its ruling is that it is an innovation, because [doing so] has not been [authentically] transmitted from the Prophet (*sal-Allaahu 'alayhe wa sallam*) and nor his Companions, so it is obligatory to leave this. The place of the intention is in the heart so there is absolutely no need to pronounce the intention.

And Allaah is the Expounder of [all] Success.

Shaykh 'Abdul-'Azeez ibn Baaz

14. Behaviour of pilgrims upon returning home after Hajj

Question: When pilgrims return from the Holy Land to their countries, some of them remain in their houses for a week without going out, not even for any necessities nor [going out to the *masjid*] to pray [in congregation]. And the people [around them] engage them in supplicating for them. So is this from the *Sunnah*?[24]

---

23 al-Bid'u wal-Muhdathaat wa maa laa Asla lahu - Page 635;
    Kitaab ad-Daw'ah - Volume 1, Page 51.

24 al-Bid'u wal-Muhdathaat wa maa laa asla lahu - Page 406.

Response: This is not from the *Sunnah*, instead it is an innovation and anyone who believes this to be a *Sunnah* is mistaken. As for them remaining in their homes without attending the congregational prayers in the *masjid*, then this is not permissible, except for a legally acceptable reason. As for what has been mentioned [above], then this is not [an] acceptable [reason], so they are sinning for not attending the [congregational] prayers.

And with Allaah lies all success and may Allaah send prayers and salutations upon our Prophet (*sal-Allaahu 'alayhe wa sallam*) and his family and his Companions.

The Permanent Committee for Islaamic Research and Verdicts

15. The two or more Khutbahs in 'Arafah

Question: We have noticed some pilgrims are unable to pray in *Masjid* Namirah[25]; They pray where they are. So one of them stands and delivers a *khutbah* and then leads the prayer, just like in a *masjid*. So, is it permissible to have two [or more] *khutbah*s in 'Arafah?[26]

Response: There is only one *khutbah* on the Day of 'Arafah, which is given by the *Imaam* of the Muslims or his deputy, in one place and that is *Masjid* Namirah. It has not been legislated for all the pilgrims, rather the remainder of the pilgrims who are unable to attend the *khutbah* should combine and shorten the *Zhuhr* and 'Asr prayers at the time of *Zhuhr* [and not delay it until 'Asr], without a *khutbah*.

14

---

25 On the 9th day of Dhul- Hijjah - the Day of 'Arafah.

26 al-Bid'u wal-Muhdathaat wa maa laa asla lahu - Page 404.

That, which these people do, as the questioner mentions, is considered an innovation and is [therefore] not permissible. Instead, it is incumbent upon them to abandon this [practice] and encourage others against it. [They should] attempt to listen to the *khutbah* [transmitted] via the speakers [placed outside *Masjid* Namirah for those unable to enter the *Masjid*].

Shaykh Saalih ibn Fowzaan

16. Touching Mihraab and Minbar of the Prophet's Masjid

Question: What is the ruling regarding touching the *mihraab* and the *minbar* of the Prophet's *Masjid?*[27]

Response: Some of the visitors touch the *mihraab* and the *minbar* and the walls of the Prophet's *Masjid* and all of this is an innovation.

Shaykh Muhammad ibn 'Uthaymeen

17. Uttering the Talbiyah as a group in chorus

Question: What is the ruling regarding uttering the *talbiyah* as a group in chorus?[28]

Response: Some of the pilgrims utter the *talbiyah* as a group in chorus; So one of them is either at the front, middle or behind and utters the *talbiyah* whilst all of them follow him in chorus. [Doing so] has not been

---

27 al-Bid'u wal-Muhdathaat wa maa laa asla lahu - Page 403.

28 al-Bid'u wal-Muhdathaat wa maa laa Asla lahu - Page 394;
    Fiqh al-'Ibaadaat - Page 343.

[authentically] transmitted on the authority of [any of] the Companions. Rather, Anas ibn Maalik (*radhi-yallaahu 'anhu*) said: 'We were with the Prophet (*sal-Allaahu 'alayhe wa sallam*) [on *Hajj al-Wadaa'* (farewell pilgrimage)] and from amongst us were those who uttered '*Allaahu Akbar*', and those who uttered '*Laa ilaaha ill-Allaah*', and others who uttered the *talbiyah*.' This is [what has been] legislated for the Muslims, whereby each one then utters the *talbiyah* on his own without joining together with others [in chorus].

Shaykh Muhammad ibn 'Uthaymeen

18. Uttering the Talbiyah in chorus

Question: What is the ruling regarding the pilgrims uttering *talbiyah* as a group [in chorus], whereby one of them utters the *talbiyah* and the rest follow him?[29]

Response: This is not permissible since no evidence exists from the Prophet (*sal-Allaahu 'alayhe wa sallam*) and nor from any of the Rightly Guided Khaleefahs [to suggest its permissibility]. Rather, it is an innovation.

And with Allaah lies all success and may Allaah send prayers and salutations upon our Prophet (*sal-Allaahu 'alayhe wa sallam*) and his family and his Companions.

The Permanent Committee for Islaamic Research and Verdicts

14

---

29 al-Bid'u wal-Muhdathaat wa maa laa Asla lahu - Page 394;
    Fataawa al-Lajnah ad-Daa.imah lil-Buhooth al-'Ilmiyyah wal-Iftaa. - Question 4, Fatwa No. 5609.

<u>Question</u>: Is the intention for undertaking the rites [of *hajj* or *'umrah*] to be verbally uttered in answering the call to pilgrimage?[30]

<u>Response</u>: [From the etiquette of] answering the call to pilgrimage is to say:

$$\text{«لَبَّيْكَ عُمْرَةً»}$$

«Here I am [in response to Your call Allaah] performing *'umrah*»[31]

...if one is intending [to perform] *'umrah*, and:

$$\text{«لَبَّيْكَ حَجّاً»}$$

«Here I am [in response to Your call Allaah] performing *hajj*»[32]

...if one is intending [to perform] *hajj*.

As for [making] the intention, then it is not permissible to verbally utter it; For example, one must not say:

"O Allaah! Indeed I intend [to perform] *'umrah*" or "...I intend [to perform] *hajj*"; This [verbal uttering of the intention] is not what the Prophet (*sal-Allaahu 'alayhe wa sallam*) did.

Shaykh Muhammad ibn 'Uthaymeen

---

30 Daleel al-Akhtaa. allaatee yaqa'a feehaa al-Haaj wal-Mu'tamir - Page 29.

31 Saheeh Muslim/214, Sunan Abee Daawood/1795, Sunan an-Nasaa.ee/2729, Sunan Ibn Maajah/2968, Musnad Ahmad/11958, Saheeh Ibn Khuzaymah/2619, Saheeh Ibn Hibbaan/3930.

32 References as listed in footnote 31.

Question: What is the ruling regarding visiting the 'Sab'ah *Masaajid*'[33] or *Masjid* al-Ghamaamah or some of the other places that some of the pilgrims frequent [during their visit to Madeenah]?[34]

Response: We [previously] mentioned that only the following five places [are legislated] to be visited [in Madeenah]:

1. The Prophet's *Masjid*;
2. His grave and the graves of his two Companions (Abu Bakr and 'Umar (*rahdi-yallaahu 'anhumaa*)), and the three graves are all in one place;
3. al-Baqee [graveyard] wherein is the grave of 'Uthmaan ibn 'Affaan (*rahdi-yallaahu 'anhu*);
4. The martyrs of [the battle of] Uhud, and amongst them the grave of Hamzah ibn 'Abdul-Muttalib (*rahdi-yallaahu 'anhu*);
5. *Masjid* Qubaa.

Any place other than these should not be visited. That which you mention of the 'Sab'ah *Masaajid*' or other than these [which you did not mention], then visiting all of these has no basis [in Islaam].

Visiting them, intending this to be a form of worship is an innovation. This is because [visiting] these have not been [authentically] transmitted on the authority of the Prophet (*sal-Allaahu 'alayhe wa sallam*). It is [therefore] not permissible for anyone to establish a time, place or

14

---

33 Also known as the 'Seven Mosques' located in the Khandaq area (where the Battle of Khandaq took place in 5 AH) in Madeenah, near the Ministry of Hajj office.

34 al-Bid'u wal-Muhdathaat wa maa laa Asla lahu - Page 400;
    Daleel al-Akhtaa. allatee yaqa'a feehaa al-Haaj wal-Mu'tamir - Page 113.

action - if done intending to draw nearness to Allaah [as a form of worship], except with evidences from the *Sharee'ah*.

Shaykh Muhammad ibn 'Uthaymeen

21. Visiting the grave of the Messenger of Allaah

Question: Are there any innovations which some people fall into [when] at the grave of the Messenger (*sal-Allaahu 'alayhe wa sallam*)?[35]

Response: From the innovations that take place at the grave of the Messenger (*sal-Allaahu 'alayhe wa sallam*) is much frequenting. For example, whenever he enters the Prophet's *Masjid*, he goes and says *salaam* to him and sits near the grave. The Prophet (*sal-Allaahu 'alayhe wa sallam*) said:

«*Do not take my grave as a place of [much] frequenting*»[36]

Rather, it is recommended for one who arrives from a journey to visit it [once].

Also, from the innovations that occur at the Messenger's grave or other than that is the assumption that the supplication there is accepted. On the contrary, it is legislated to send salutations upon him (*sal-Allaahu*

---

35 al-Bid'u wal-Muhdathaat wa maa laa Asla lahu - Page 240;
    Majallah ad-Da'wah - No.1612, Page 37.

36 Sunan Abee Daawood/2042, Musannaf 'Abdir-Razzaaq/6726, Musannaf Ibn Abee Shaybah/7542, Musnad Ahmad/8804, Musnad al-Bazzaar/509, Musnad Abee Ya'laa/469.

'alayhe wa sallam), and if he wants to supplicate then it is [to be] done in any part of the *Masjid*, and if it is done after the prayer then that is best. From that which is done and disliked at the grave of the Prophet (*sal-Allaahu 'alayhe wa sallam*) is raising the voice and requesting from him (*sal-Allaahu 'alayhe wa sallam*) that one's needs be satisfied. This is major *shirk*, and it is obligatory to beware of it.

Shaykh Saalih ibn Fowzaan

22. Washing the stones for stoning the Jamaraat pillars

Question: What is the ruling regarding washing the stones for stoning [the *jamaraat* pillars]?[37]

Response: They should not be washed. Rather, if a person washes them with the intention of worshipping Allaah [by this action], then this is an innovation because the Prophet (*sal-Allaahu 'alayhe wa sallam*) did not do this.

Shaykh Muhammad ibn 'Uthaymeen

23. When the day of 'Arafah coincides with a Friday

Question: Some people say that if the day of 'Arafah[38] falls on a Friday, then it is as if someone has performed 7 *hajj*'s[39]. Is there any evidence

14

---

37 al-Bid'u wal-Muhdathaat wa maa laa asla lahu - Page 404;
    Fataawa al-Hajj wal-'Umrah - Page 53.

38 9 Dhul-Hijjah.

39 i.e. he is rewarded as having done so.

from the *Sunnah* regarding this?[40]

Response: There is no authentic evidence regarding this. [However], some people [also] believe this equates to [having performed] 70 *hajj*'s or 72 *hajj*'s, and this is also incorrect.

And with Allaah lies all success and may Allaah send prayers and salutations upon our Prophet (*sal-Allaahu 'alayhe wa sallam*) and his family and his Companions.

The Permanent Committee for Islaamic Research and Verdicts

---

40 Fataawa al-Lajnah ad-Daa.imah lil-Buhooth al-'Ilmiyyah wal-Iftaa. - Volume 11, Page 211, Question 3 of Fatwa No.7890.

Chapter Fifteen

Miscellaneous Issues

1. Advice to those having performed the Hajj

<u>Question</u>: What is your advice to the one who has performed the obligatory [first] *hajj*?[1]

<u>Response</u>: My advice is that he should fear Allaah [and always be conscious of Him] when performing all that which Allaah has obligated upon him in terms of other acts of worship such as *salaah, zakaah,* fasting, honouring the parents, enjoining family ties and being good to the creation [of Allaah], and to the animals under ones ownership and other than this from that which Allaah has commanded with. That which encompasses all of this is the statement of Allaah:

1 Daleel al-Akhtaa.a yaqa'a feehaa al-Haaj wal-Mu'tamir wat-tahdtheer minhaa - Page 117;
Fataawa al-Hajj wal-'Umrah - Page 120-121.

إِنَّ ٱللَّهَ يَأْمُرُ بِٱلْعَدْلِ
وَٱلْإِحْسَٰنِ وَإِيتَآئِ ذِى ٱلْقُرْبَىٰ وَيَنْهَىٰ عَنِ ٱلْفَحْشَآءِ
وَٱلْمُنكَرِ وَٱلْبَغْىِ يَعِظُكُمْ لَعَلَّكُمْ تَذَكَّرُونَ
(٩٠) وَأَوْفُوا۟ بِعَهْدِ ٱللَّهِ إِذَا عَٰهَدتُّمْ وَلَا تَنقُضُوا۟ ٱلْأَيْمَٰنَ
بَعْدَ تَوْكِيدِهَا وَقَدْ جَعَلْتُمُ ٱللَّهَ عَلَيْكُمْ كَفِيلًا إِنَّ
ٱللَّهَ يَعْلَمُ مَا تَفْعَلُونَ

Verily, Allaah enjoins al-'Adl (justice) and al-Ih-saan (being patient in performing one's duties to Allaah), and giving (help) to kith and kin: and forbids al-Fahshaa. (all evil deeds), and al-Munkar (all that is prohibited), and al-Baghee (all kinds of oppression), He admonishes you, that you may take heed. And fulfill the Covenant of Allaah (Bay'ah: pledge for Islaam) when you have covenanted, and break not the oaths after you have confirmed them, and indeed you have appointed Allaah your surety. Verily! Allaah knows what you do.[2]

Shaykh Muhammad ibn 'Uthaymeen

2. Appointing an ameer during Hajj journey

Question: Is our appointing an *ameer* during our *hajj* journey permis-

---

2 The Noble Qur.aan - Soorah an-Nahl, Aayahs 90-91.

sible or not?[3]

Response: Whilst travelling, it has been legislated for a group, if they are three or more [in number] that they appoint an *ameer* from amongst themselves. It is mentioned in the *Sunan* of Abu Daawood on the authority of Abu Sa'eed al-Khudree (*radhi-yallaahu 'anhu*) that the Messenger of Allaah (*sal-Allaahu 'alayhe wa sallam*) said:

«*If three depart on a journey, then one of them must lead[4] them*»[5]

And with that, they should combine their affairs, and should not be divided in their decisions, and nor should there be any conflict between them.

And with Allaah lies all success and may Allaah send prayers and salutations upon our Prophet (*sal-Allaahu 'alayhe wa sallam*) and his family and his Companions.

The Permanent Committee for Islaamic Research and Verdicts

3. Argument and quarrelling during Hajj

Question: If there occurs argumenting and quarrelling between a man and his companions during *hajj*, would his *hajj* still be valid, and will it

---

3 Fataawa al-Lajnah ad-Daa.imah lil-Buhooth al-'Ilmiyyah wal-Iftaa. - Volume 11, Page 110, Question 1 of Fatwa No.12084.

4 i.e. be the ameer.

5 Sunan Abee Daawood/2608, Sharhus-Sunnah lil-Baghawee/2676.

be rewarded even if it was his obligatory [first] *hajj*?[6]

Response: His *hajj* is valid and will [*inshaa.-Allaah*] be rewarded as his obligatory [first] *hajj*, however, his reward will be reduced according to the severity of the ugly altercation which took place. So it is upon him to repent [to Allaah] for that, as Allaah (*Subhaanahu wa Ta'aala*) says:

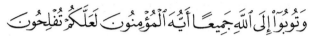

And all of you beg Allaah to forgive you all, O believers, that you may be successful[7]

And with Allaah lies all success and may Allaah send prayers and salutations upon our Prophet (*sal-Allaahu 'alayhe wa sallam*) and his family and his Companions.

The Permanent Committee for Islaamic Research and Verdicts

4. Best time for 'Umrah

Question: Has the excellence of performing *'umrah* specifically during the months of *hajj*[8] been established over and above its excellence during other months?[9]

Response: The best time to perform *'umrah* is in the month of *Ramad-*

---

6 Fataawa al-Lajnah ad-Daa.imah lil-Buhooth al-'Ilmiyyah wal-Iftaa. - Volume 11, Page 112, Question 2 of Fatwa No.9892.

7 The Noble Qur.aan - Soorah an-Noor, Aayah 31.

8 Shawwaal, Dhul-Qi'dah and the first ten days of Dhul-Hijjah.

9 Fataawa al-Hajj wal-'Umrah waz-Ziyaarah - Pages 133-134.

haan, because the Prophet (*sal-Allaahu 'alayhe wa sallam*) said:

«*'Umrah in Ramadhaan is equivalent to hajj*»[10]

And in another narration:

«*...is equivalent to doing hajj with me*»[11]

And in [yet] another narration:

«*...is equivalent to doing hajj or hajj with me*»[12]

It was transmitted like this evoking uncertainty, implying with Him (*sal-Allaahu 'alayhe wa sallam*).

Thereafter, performing the *'umrah* in *Dhul-Qi'dah* [is best] because all the *'umrah*s performed by Him (*sal-Allaahu 'alayhe wa sallam*) were done so in *Dhul-Qi'dah* - and the excellence of doing as He (*sal-Allaahu 'alayhe wa sallam*) did is in accordance with the statement of Allaah:

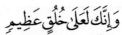

And verily, you (O Muhammad) are on an exalted

---

10 Saheeh al-Bukhaaree/1782, Sunan Abee Daawood/1988, Sunan at-Tirmidhee/939, Sunan Ibn Maajah/2991, Musnad Ibn Abee Shaybah/771, Musnad Ahmad/2808, Sunan ad-Daarimee/1901, Musnad al-Bazzaar/636, Saheeh ibn Hibbaan/3075.

11 Saheeh al-Bukhaaree/1863, al-Mu'jam al-Kabeer lit-Tabaraanee/11299, al-Musnad al-Mustakhraj 'alaa Saheeh Muslim li-Abee Na'eem/2901, Mawaarid ath-Thamaan ilaa Zawaa.id Ibn Hibbaan/1020.

12 References as listed in footnote 11.

15

(standard of) character.[13]

And with Allaah lies all success.

Shaykh 'Abdul-'Azeez ibn Baaz

5. Did not visit the Prophet's Masjid

Question: I visited Makkah al-Mukarramah in the month of *Ramadhaan* intending to perform *'umrah*. However, a day after arriving in Makkah al-Mukarramah I became ill and was unable to complete the rituals of *'umrah*; [All] I [was able to do was to] complete the *tawaaf* around the *Ka'bah* seven times, and then walk between *Safaa* and *Marwah*, but was unable to travel to Madeenah to visit the Prophet's *Masjid* since I was ill. So I returned back to my country. Will this visit of ours be considered an *'umrah*?[14]

Response: If you performed *tawaaf* and *sa'ee*, and [thereafter] cut your hair, then you have completed your *'umrah* and therein [*inshaa.-Allaah*] is the reward. As for visiting Madeenah, then this is not an integral part of the *'umrah* - [in fact] it has nothing to do with the *'umrah*; Rather, visiting the Prophet's *Masjid* is recommended for the Muslim whenever he is able to do so.

Shaykh Muhammad ibn 'Uthaymeen

---

13 The Noble Qur.aan - Soorah al-Qalam, Aayah 4.

14 Fataawa al-Hajj wal-'Umrah waz-Ziyaarah - Page 142.

6. Hajj or donate money to Muslims in Chechnya

Question: If someone has saved up money to perform their very first *hajj*, would it be better to donate this money to our Muslim brothers and sisters in Chechnya or go ahead and perform *hajj?*[15]

Response: It is better to perform the [first] *hajj* which is obligatory upon the Muslim.

Shaykh Muhammad ibn 'Uthaymeen

7. Donating the allocated funds for a voluntary Hajj

Question: I have performed my obligatory [first] *hajj*; [Since] I am wealthy - should I donate funds allocated for a second *hajj* or should I actually go and perform the *hajj?*[16]

Response: If you have plenty of money and are thereby able to donate [funds in charity] as well as go and perform [a voluntary] *hajj*, then that is best. If however you are unable to do so, and you are aware of the poor and needy who are in desperate need [for donations] or there is a charitable project which needs funds, then it is better to donate the funds there instead of performing [a voluntary] *hajj* for another time; If however there is no desperate need for funds, then performing the [voluntary] *hajj* is better.

Shaykh 'Abdullaah ibn Jibreen

15

---

15 Question put to the Shaykh after Fajr in al-Masjid al-Haraam in Makkah on Tuesday 27 Ramadhaan 1420/ 4 January 2000.

16 Fataawa al-Hajj wal-'Umrah waz-Ziyaarah - Pages 144-145.

8. Hajj or donate money to mujaahideen in Afghanistan

Question: Regarding the one who has already performed the obligatory [first] *hajj*, and [now] Allaah has facilitated for him to perform *hajj* a second time, is it permissible for him to donate the amount he would spend on performing *hajj* to the Muslim *mujaahideen* in Afghanistan or other than them - since the *hajj* would be voluntary and donating [funds] for *jihaad* is obligatory. [Please] advise us, [and] may Allaah reward you with much good?[17]

Response: If the questioner is saying that the second *hajj* is voluntary and exerting [oneself] for *jihaad* is obligatory, then the outcome of that is that he has ruled for himself that donating [the funds] for *jihaad* is better, because it is obligatory since one is sinning by not doing so - according to his statement. Rather, that which I am of the opinion is that the *jihaad* in Afghanistan is not obligatory upon everyone, however, I am also of the opinion that to generously donate money towards it [*jihaad*] is better than spending it on a voluntary *hajj*, because the voluntary *jihaad* is better than the voluntary *hajj*.

Shaykh Muhammad ibn 'Uthaymeen

9. Go to Makkah or travel to other countries for Da'wah

Question: During the last part of *Ramadhaan*, which is better to do: Going to Makkah and remaining there for the rest of *Ramadhaan* or travelling to some countries which are in need of *da'wah* and education?[18]

---

17   Fataawa ash-Shaykh Muhammad as-Saalih al-'Uthaymeen - Volume 2, Page 677.

18   Fataawa as-Siyaam libni Jibreen - Page 176, Fatwa No.193.

Response: Our opinion is that travelling for the purpose of *da'wah* is preferable for whoever possesses the ability to do so and in turn benefiting the people who are surrounded by ignorance (lack of knowledge) and [who] persist in falsehood, since no one comes to them to call them [to the truth]. However, if a person does not have the ability to travel because he is poor or does not have the ability to give *da'wah* as he has no knowledge to resolve the doubts and uncertainties, then [remaining and increasing in] worship is better for him, either in Makkah or elsewhere.

Shaykh 'Abdullaah ibn Jibreen

10. Looking at women during Hajj

Question: What is the ruling regarding looking at women during *hajj*?[19]

Response: Looking at women for whom you are not a *mahram* is prohibited during *hajj* and other than it; However, its [level of] prohibition is greater during *hajj*.

Shaykh 'Abdul-'Azeez Aal ash-Shaykh

11. Lost property found in Makkah

Question: Is it permissible for me to pick up lost property in Makkah [upon finding it] and go to the area where I live and make an announcement about it, or am I required to make an announcement by the doors of the *masaajid* and the markets and elsewhere in Makkah?[20]

---

19 ad-Durar an-Naadhirah fil-Fataawa al-Mu'aasirah - Page 451;
   'Abdul-'Azeez Aal ash-Shaykh - ad-Da'wah 1543, Muharram 1417AH.

20 Fataawa al-Hajj wal-'Umrah waz-Ziyaarah - Page 141.

Response: The lost property [found] in Makkah is characterised by the fact that it is not permissible for anyone to pick it up unless they plan on making an announcement about it until they find the owner, or they plan on handing it to the officially appointed lost property representative (office), because the Prophet (*sal-Allaahu 'alayhe wa sallam*) said:

«It is not permissible to pick up lost property except for the one who wants to announce it».[21]

And the wisdom behind that is - if the lost property was left in it's place, then its owner will probably return to it and find it there. So based upon this, we say to this brother - you are required to make an announcement about it in Makkah al-Mukarramah, in and around the place where you found it - such as the doors of the *masaajid* and the gatherings, otherwise you must hand it in to the officially appointed lost property representative (office).

Shaykh Muhammad ibn 'Uthaymeen

12. Law requires shaving off beard to renew passport

Question: Your excellency, my passport has expired and I want to renew it so that I can come and perform *'umrah* and the obligatory [first] *hajj*. [The passport office] requested I shave off my beard in accordance with the new law which was recently passed in my country. So what do I do? And may Allaah reward you with good.[22]

---

21 Saheeh al-Bukhaaree/2433 and 4313, Sunan Abee Daawood/2017, Sunan an-Nasaa.ee/2892.

22 Silsilah Kitaab ad-Da'wah (10), al-Fataawa - Volume 3, Page 42.

Response: In the Name of Allaah, and all Praise is for Allaah [alone]. We advise you not to adhere [to their request] to shave off your beard, rather, be patient until another time, and Allaah will make an opening for you [and facilitate for you your affairs], as He (*Subhaanahu wa Ta'aala*) says:

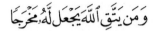

> **And whosoever fears Allaah and keeps his duty to Him, He will make a way for him to get out (from every difficulty)**[23]

And from that which is known, the shaving off of the beard is a sin, because the Prophet (*sal-Allaahu 'alayhe wa sallam*) commanded [the men] to leave [their] beards to grow. And it is authenticated from him (*sal-Allaahu 'alayhe wa sallam*) that he said:

> «**Indeed, obedience is in (all) that is good, (and) there is no obedience to (any of) the creation whilst committing a sin against Allaah**»[24]

And may Allaah grant everyone success.

Shaykh 'Abdul-'Azeez ibn Baaz

---

23 The Noble Qur.aan - Soorah at-Talaaq, Aayah 2.

24 Saheeh Muslim/39, Sunan Abee Daawood/2625, Sunan an-Nasaa.ee/4205, Saheeh Ibn Hibbaan/4567, as-Sunan al-Kubraa lil-Bayhaqee/16609;
And in another hadeeth it mentions: «*There is no obedience to (any of) the creation whilst committing a sin against Allaah*» - Musannaf Ibn Abee Shaybah/33717, Musnad al-Bazzaar/1988, al-Mu'jam al-Kabeer lit-Tabaraanee/381, Sharhus-Sunnah lil-Baghawee/2455.

13. Overcrowding during the Hajj

Question: [Some] people intentionally overcrowd when performing some of the rites of *hajj*, so is their *hajj* valid or invalid?[25]

Response: Their *hajj* is not invalidated by overcrowding. However, they are sinful if they intentionally sought to do so without cause or reason - since this entails oppression and harm towards the [other] pilgrims and causing them to be put off from *hajj*.

If, however, a person was forced [to overcrowd] without intending [so], rather as a result of overcrowding by others around him, then *inshaa.-Allaah* there is no harm [or penalty] upon him as Allaah (*'Azza wa Jall*) says:

فَٱتَّقُوا۟ ٱللَّهَ مَا ٱسْتَطَعْتُمْ

So fear Allaah as much as you are able[26]

And He (*'Azza wa Jall*) says:

لَا يُكَلِّفُ ٱللَّهُ نَفْسًا إِلَّا وُسْعَهَا

Allaah burdens not a person beyond his scope[27]

And Allaah is the Expounder of All Success.

Shaykh 'Abdul-'Azeez ibn Baaz

---

25 Fataawa al-Hajj wal-'Umrah waz-Ziyaarah - Page 11.

26 The Noble Qur.aan - Soorah at-Taghaabun, Aayah 16.

27 The Noble Qur.aan - Soorah al-Baqarah, Aayah 286.

14. Shortening the Prayers in Makkah

Question: What is the ruling regarding the pilgrim shortening the [obligatory] prayers throughout his stay in Makkah beyond four days?[28]

Response: If the duration of the stay of the pilgrim is four days or less, then it is recommended for him to shorten his four *rak'ah* prayers to two *rak'ah*s; This is in accordance with the example of the Prophet (*sal-Allaahu 'alayhe wa sallam*) during his farewell *hajj*. If however he intends on remaining [in Makkah] longer than four days, then he is required to pray [the full] four *rak'ah*s - and this is the opinion of the majority of the people of knowledge.

Shaykh 'Abdul-'Azeez ibn Baaz

15. Special characteristics of Zam Zam water

Question: What are the special characteristics of *Zam Zam* water?[29]

Response: From the special characteristics of *Zam Zam* water is that the Prophet (*sal-Allaahu 'alayhe wa sallam*) said:

«Zam Zam water is for what it is drunk for»[30]

So when a person drinks it to quench his thirst, it is quenched, and when he drinks it to satisfy his hunger, it is satisfied; So these are [amongst]

---

the special characteristics of *Zam Zam* water.

Shaykh Muhammad ibn 'Uthaymeen

16. Stopped praying after Hajj

Question: A person performed the obligatory *hajj* and afterwards he abandoned the prayer - and refuge is sought in Allaah; He then repented and began to perform the prayer. So is it obligatory for him to perform *hajj* again, considering he had abandoned the prayer and the one who abandons the prayer is a *kaafir*? We anticipate [your] guidance [on this matter and] may Allaah reward you [with good].[31]

Response: If the situation is as the questioner mentions, then his *hajj* is not nullified and he is not required to perform another *hajj* because righteous actions are only nullified if one dies upon disbelief [*kufr*]. However, if Allaah guided him and he accepted Islaam and died upon Islaam, then indeed for him is what has preceded from [his] good [actions], for that which Allaah (*'Azza wa Jall*) says:

$$\text{وَمَن يَرْتَدِدْ}$$

$$\text{مِنكُمْ عَن دِينِهِ فَيَمُتْ وَهُوَ كَافِرٌ فَأُوْلَئِكَ حَبِطَتْ}$$
$$\text{أَعْمَالُهُمْ فِي ٱلدُّنْيَا وَٱلْآخِرَةِ وَأُوْلَئِكَ أَصْحَابُ ٱلنَّارِ}$$

And whosoever of you turns back from his religion and dies as a disbeliever, then his deeds will be lost in this life and in the Hereafter, and they will be the dwellers of the Fire.[32]

---

31 Majmoo' Fataawa wa Maqaalaat Mutanawwi'ah - Volume 16, Page 373.

32 The Noble Qur.aan - Soorah al-Baqarah, Aayah 217.

...and for what he (sal-Allaahu 'alayhe wa sallam said to Hakeem ibn Hizaam when he asked him about his righteous actions he did during [the time of] ignorance [before he embraced Islaam], will they benefit him in the Hereafter? So he (sal-Allaahu 'alayhe wa sallam) said to him:

«*You embraced Islaam upon what has passed you from good [actions]*»[33]

And Allaah is the Expounder of all success.

Shaykh 'Abdul-'Azeez ibn Baaz

17. The effects of Hajj upon the Muslim

Question: What are the effects of *hajj* upon the Muslim?

Response: We have previously mentioned something in this regard when I was asked: What are the signs of an accepted *hajj*?[34]

So, from the effects of *hajj* upon the Muslim is that he will notice within himself calmness and tranquility, as well as delight and pleasure, and enlightenment of the heart.

In addition, from amongst the effects of *hajj*: It is possible the Muslim gains from beneficial knowledge which he hears in the lessons and gatherings held in *al-Masjid al-Haraam* as well as the tents in Minaa and 'Arafah.

15

---

33 Saheeh al-Bukhaaree/1436, Saheeh Muslim/123.

34 Fataawa al-Hajj wal-'Umrah - Page 119-120.

In addition, from amongst the effects of *hajj*: The Muslim will increase in his knowledge and understanding of the state of affairs of the Muslims around the world, if he is fortunate to meet someone who tells him about them.

In addition, from amongst the effects of *hajj*: The instilling of love in the hearts of the believers for one another; Certainly you will find the Muslim during *hajj* - signs of guidance and uprightness will be emanating from him - and as such, you will love him and there will settle in your heart a bond [of brotherhood towards each other].

And from amongst the effects of *hajj*: The Muslim may benefit financially in his trading and otherwise, as Allaah (*Subhaanahu wa Ta'aala*) says:

لِّيَشْهَدُواْ
مَنَٰفِعَ لَهُمْ وَيَذْكُرُواْ ٱسْمَ ٱللَّهِ فِيٓ أَيَّامٍ مَّعْلُومَٰتٍ
عَلَىٰ مَا رَزَقَهُم مِّنۢ بَهِيمَةِ ٱلْأَنْعَٰمِ

That they may witness things that are of benefit to them, and mention the Name of Allaah on appointed days, over the beast of cattle that He has provided for them...[35]

And He (*Subhaanahu wa Ta'aala*) says:

لَيْسَ عَلَيْكُمْ جُنَاحٌ أَن تَبْتَغُواْ فَضْلًا مِّن رَّبِّكُمْ

There is no sin on you if you seek the bounty of

---

35 The Noble Qur.aan - Soorah al-Hajj, Aayah 28.

And how many Muslims have gained financially by trading during their *hajj* - buying and selling - and these are from the benefits which Allaah (*Subhaanahu wa Ta'aala*) has mentioned.

And from amongst the effects of *hajj*: The Muslim habituates himself with patience towards hardship and inconvenience, particularly if he is a normal (not wealthy) person - unlike those who experience much comfort and luxury during their *hajj* - then indeed he will benefit immensely in that regard. I mean, whoever's *hajj* is normal (without comfort and luxury), then he will benefit immensely by habituating himself with patience towards hardship and inconvenience.

Shaykh Muhammad ibn 'Uthaymeen

18. The signs of an accepted Hajj or 'Umrah

Question: Are there any signs which appear upon those whose performance of *hajj* or *'umrah* is accepted?[37]

Response: It is possible for there to be signs for the one whose *hajj*, fasting, charity or prayer has been accepted by Allaah and they are: the opening of the heart [to good], happiness of the heart and a lighted face. Certainly, for worshipping [Allaah] there are signs that appear on the body, signs that are visible and signs that are hidden. Some of the

15

---

36 The Noble Qur.aan - Soorah al-Baqarah, Aayah 198.

37 Daleel al-Akhtaa.a yaqa'a feehaa al-Haaj wal-Mu'tamir wat-tahdtheer minhaa - Page 115;
Fataawaa al-Hajj wal-'Umrah - Page 118-119.

Pious Predecessors have mentioned that from the signs that [a] good [act] has been accepted [by Allaah] is that he will be granted the *towfeeq* to do [yet] another good [act]. Certainly the *towfeeq* of Allaah for him to do more good [acts] after it, is evidence that Allaah (*'Azza wa Jall*) has accepted his previous good [acts]. He has made it easy for him to do another good act and is happy with him for it.

Shaykh Muhammad ibn 'Uthaymeen

19. Want to do Hajj but did not fast in Ramadhaan

Question: I became ill in the blessed month of *Ramadhaan* and was unable to fast at the time. So I decided to fast later when I become better - so long as Allaah grants me life. Now the time for *hajj* is upon us and I want to perform *hajj* this year. Would it be permissible for me to perform *hajj* [this year] since I did not fast [in *Ramadhaan*]?[38]

Response: It is permissible for you to perform *hajj* - even if you have not yet made up the missed fasts of *Ramadhaan*. However, so long as you are able, it is not permissible for you to delay making up [the missed fasts] until the arrival of the following *Ramadhaan*.

And with Allaah lies all success and may Allaah send prayers and salutations upon our Prophet (*sal-Allaahu 'alayhe wa sallam*) and his family and his Companions.

The Permanent Committee for Islaamic Research and Verdicts

---

38 Fataawa al-Hajj wal-'Umrah waz-Ziyaarah - Page 138.

20. Wife pays for Husband's 'Umrah expenses

Question: A wife volunteered to pay for the expenses of an 'umrah for her husband, from her own money as a gift to him. Bearing in mind he is capable of performing 'umrah from his own money, is there any religious issues related to this act [of hers towards her husband]? Provide us with a legal ruling regarding this, and may you be rewarded, inshaa.-Allaah.[39]

Response: There is no harm in this, and may Allaah reward her with good for her [noble] gesture; This is because it is considered as assisting one another upon righteousness and piety.

Shaykh 'Abdul-'Azeez ibn Baaz

---

39 Fataawa al-Hajj wal-'Umrah waz-Ziyaarah - Page 128.

Appendix I

"Simple Hajj Guide"

This "Simple Hajj Guide"[1] has been produced using the book "Manaasik al-Hajj wal-'Umrah" of Shaykh Muhammad Naasiruddeen al-Albaanee.

Upon arrival in Makkah	- **'Umrah (Tawaaf al-Qudoom)**
8th Dhul-Hijjah	- **Ihraam**
	Stay in Minaa
9th Dhul-Hijjah	- **Stand in 'Arafah**
	Stay in Muzdalifah
10th Dhul-Hijjah	- **Stoning**
	Sacrifice
	Shave Head
	Tawaaf al-Ifaadhah
11th, 12th, 13th Dhul-Hijjah	- **Stay in Minaa for Stoning**
Upon departure from Makkah	- **Tawaaf al-Wadaa'**

---

1 A single A4 sheet foldable pocket version of this "Simple Hajj Guide" is available for free download from http://www.fatwa-online.com

1. 'Umrah (Tawaaf al-Qudoom)

Proceed to appropriate Meeqaat. On entering state of Ihraam recite -

لَبَّيْكَ اللَّهُمَّ بِعُمْرَة

Here I am O Allaah, (in response to Your call) making 'Umrah.

In fear of not completing the 'Umrah, recite -

اللَّهُمَّ مَحِلِّيْ حَيْثُ حَبَسْتَنِي

O Allaah, [If I am prevented by an obstacle then indeed] my place is where You prevent me.

Standing, face the Qiblah and recite -

اللَّهُمَّ هَذِهِ عُمْرَةٌ لاَ رِيَاءَ فِيْهَا وَلاَ سُمْعَة

O Allaah, there is no showing off nor seeking repute in this 'Umrah.

Then loudly recite the talbiyah -

لَبَّيْكَ اللَّهُمَّ لَبَّيْك، لَبَّيْكَ لاَ شَرِيْكَ لَكَ لَبَّيْك
إِنَّ الْحَمْدَ وَ النِّعْمَةَ لَكَ وَ الْمُلْكُ لاَ شَرِيْكَ لَك

Here I am O Allaah, (in response to Your call), here I am. Here I am, You have no partner, here I am. Indeed all the Praise, Grace & Sovereignty belong to You. You have no partner.

211

...also from the talbiyah, recite -

لَبَّيْكَ إِلَهَ الْحَقِّ

Here I am O Lord of Truth.

Upon entering al-Masjid al-Haraam with the right foot, recite -

اللَّهُمَّ صَلِّ عَلَى مُحَمَّدٍ وَ سَلِّم

اللَّهُمَّ افْتَحْ لِي أَبْوَابَ رَحْمَتِك

O Allaah, send prayers & peace upon Muhammad,
O Allaah, open the doors of Your Mercy for me.

Starting at al-Hajar al-Aswad[2], men only - uncover right shoulder by placing Ihraam underneath right arm-pit. When beginning each circuit, make a sign with your right hand towards al-Hajar al-Aswad[3], and recite -

Allaah is the Greatest.

---

2 If possible, cling to area between the corner of al-Hajar al-Aswad & the door, placing the chest, face & forearms upon this area.

3 If possible, touch al-Hajar al-Aswad with the right hand & also kiss al-Hajar al-Aswad, then prostrate on it - this is best; if not, then touch it with the right hand then kiss the right hand; if not, simply make a sign towards it with the right hand.

Make seven circuit's of Ka'bah[4] (for first three circuit's only, men only swiftly walk around the Ka'bah; Then begin fourth circuit, walking at normal pace completely around & finish until seventh circuit). During each circuit, whilst between ar-Rukn al-Yamaanee[5] & al-Hajar al-Aswad, recite -

$$\{ رَبَّنَا آتِنَا فِي الدُّنْيَا حَسَنَةً وَ فِي الآخِرَةِ حَسَنَةً وَ قِنَا عَذَابَ النَّارِ \}$$

Our Lord! Give us in this world that which is good & in the Hereafter that which is good, and save us from the torment of the Fire!

Cover right shoulder, then go behind Station of Ibraaheem and recite -

$$\{ وَاتَّخِذُوْا مِنْ مَّقَامِ إِبْرَاهِيْمَ مُصَلَّى \}$$

And take the station of Ibraaheem as a place of prayer.

Behind Station of Ibraaheem - if possible, otherwise anywhere within al-Masjid al-Haraam: Pray two rak'ah naafilah; In first rak'ah recite Soorah al-Kaafiroon & in second rak'ah, Soorah al-Ikhlaas. Then go to Zam-Zam well & drink from it, then pour some water over head. Return to al-Hajar

---

4 There is no specific du'aa during the walk around the Ka'bah, apart from what has been mentioned for between ar-Rukn al-Yamaanee to al-Hajar al-Aswad. You can therefore recite the Qur.aan or any du'aa as you please.

5 If possible, touch ar-Rukn al-Yamaanee each time (but do not kiss it) - this is best; if not, then do not make any sign towards it.

al-Aswad & make a sign with your right hand towards it for the last time[6], & recite -

الله أَكْبَر

Allaah is the Greatest.

Begin Sa'ee at as-Safaa. At foot of as-Safaa recite -

{إِنَّ الصَّفَا وَالْمَرْوَةَ مِنْ شَعَائِرِ الله فَمَنْ
حَجَّ الْبَيْتَ أَوِ اعْتَمَرَ فَلاَ جُنَاحَ عَلَيْهِ أَنْ يَطَّوَّفَ
بِهِمَا وَمَنْ تَطَوَّعَ خَيْراً فَإِنَّ الله شَاكِرٌ عَلِيْم}
نَبْدَأُ بِمَا بَدَأَ الله به

Verily! as-Safaa & al-Marwah are of the Symbols of Allaah. So it is not a sin on him who performs Hajj or 'Umrah of the House to perform the

Tawaaf between them. And whoever does good voluntarily, then verily, Allaah is All-Recogniser, All-Knower. We begin with what Allaah began with.

Each time upon as-Safaa and al-Marwah facing Ka'bah, recite -

---

6 If possible, touch al-Hajar al-Aswad with the right hand & also kiss al-Hajar al-Aswad, then prostrate on it - this is best; if not, then touch it with the right hand then kiss the right hand; if not, simply make a sign towards it with the right hand.

اللهُ أَكْبَر، اللهُ أَكْبَر، اللهُ أَكْبَر

لاَ إِلَهَ إِلاَّ اللهُ وَحْدَهُ لاَ شَرِيْكَ لَه، لَهُ الْمُلْكُ وَ

لَهُ الْحَمْدُ يُحْيِي وَ يُمِيْتُ وَ هُوَ عَلَى كُلِّ شَيْءٍ

قَدِيرٌ؛ لاَ إِلَهَ إِلاَّ اللهُ وَحْدَهُ لاَ شَرِيْكَ لَه، أَنْجَزَ

وَعْدَهُ وَ نَصَرَ عَبْدَهُ وَ هَزَمَ الأَحْزَابَ وَ حْدَه

Allaah is the Greatest, Allaah is the Greatest, Allaah is the Greatest. There is none truly worthy of worship except Allaah alone, without partner. To Him belongs all Sovereignty & all Praise. He alone gives life & causes death, He is Omnipotent over all things. There is none truly worthy of worship except Allaah alone, without partner. He has fulfilled His promise, & helped His slave, & He alone has defeated the confederates.

- three times, making du'aa after first & second recitation only.

Between the walk from as-Safaa to al-Marwah & al-Marwah to as-Safaa, it is permissable to recite -

رَبِّ اغْفِرْ وَارْحَمْ، إِنَّكَ أَنْتَ الأَعَزُّ الأَكْرَم

O Lord forgive me & have mercy, verily You are the Mightiest & Noblest.

Complete walk from as-Safaa to al-Marwah (one circuit), then al-Marwah to as-Safaa (second circuit) & continue for seven circuits, finishing at al-Marwah. Upon encountering green lights, men only - run from one light to other light.

Upon leaving al-Masjid al-Haraam with the left foot, recite -

$$ اللّٰهُمَّ صَلِّ عَلَى مُحَمَّدٍ وَ سَلِّم $$

$$ اللّٰهُمَّ إِنِّي أَسْأَلُكَ مِنْ فَضْلِكَ $$

O Allaah, send prayers & peace upon Muhammad,
O Allaah, verily I ask You from Your Favour.

Finally, men: cut hair equally from all over head - best, or shave head; women: cut one-third finger length of hair.

Remove Ihraam, as all restrictions are now lifted - & await morning of 8th of Dhul-Hijjah.

2. 8th day of Dhul-Hijjah (Yawm at-Tarwiyah)

Between the time period of after Fajr until before Zhuhr:

Ihraam

Enter state of Ihraam[7]; Make intention for Hajj, reciting -

$$ لَبَّيْكَ اللّٰهُمَّ بِحَجّ $$

Here I am O Allaah, (in response to Your call) mak-ing Hajj.

---

7 From wherever you are residing - hotel, house, etc.

In fear of not completing the Hajj, recite -

اللَّهُمَّ مَحِلِّي حَيْثُ حَبَسْتَنِي

O Allaah, [If I am prevented by an obstacle then indeed] my place is where You prevent me.

Standing, face the Qiblah & recite -

اللَّهُمَّ هَذِهِ حَجَّةٌ لاَ رِيَاءَ فِيْهَا وَلاَ سُمْعَة

O Allaah, there is no showing off nor seeking repute in this Hajj.

Then loudly recite the talbiyah -

لَبَّيْكَ اللَّهُمَّ لَبَّيْك، لَبَّيْكَ لاَ شَرِيْكَ لَكَ لَبَّيْك

إِنَّ الْحَمْدَ وَ النِّعْمَةَ لَكَ وَ الْمُلْكُ لاَ شَرِيْكَ لَك

Here I am O Allaah, (in response to Your call), here I am. Here I am, You have no partner, here I am. Indeed all the Praise, Grace & Sovereignty belong to You. You have no partner.

also from the talbiyah, recite -

لَبَّيْكَ إِلَهَ الْحَقّ

Here I am O Lord of Truth.

Calmly proceed to Minaa - pray Zhuhr, 'Asr, Maghrib & 'Ishaa in shortened form but not combined[8].

3. 9th day of Dhul-Hijjah (Yawm 'Arafah)

Stand in 'Arafah

Pray Fajr, then, after sunrise, calmly proceed to 'Arafah. It is permissible
to continue to recite the talbiyah -

لَبَّيْكَ اللَّهُمَّ لَبَّيْك، لَبَّيْكَ لاَ شَرِيْكَ لَكَ لَبَّيْك

إِنَّ الْحَمْدَ وَ النِّعْمَةَ لَكَ وَ الْمُلْكُ لاَ شَرِيْكَ لَك

*Here I am O Allaah, (in response to Your call), here
I am. Here I am, You have no partner, here I am.
Indeed all the Praise, Grace & Sovereignty belong
to You. You have no partner.*

and also proclaim the Greatness of Allaah by reciting -

Allaah is the Greatest.

---

8 Pray two Fard each for Zhuhr, 'Asr & 'Ishaa. Maghrib is not shortened, & remains
three Fard. 'Ishaa to be followed by Witr.

Stopover at Namirah[9] & remain there until after Zawaal (sun at highest point - no shadow). Then calmly proceed to 'Uranah[10] & listen to the Khutbah. At the time of Zhuhr, pray Zhuhr & 'Asr (in shortened form & combined), after one Adhaan & two Iqaamah's. Do not pray anything between these two prayers, nor pray anything after 'Asr.

Then calmly proceed to 'Arafah, remaining there until sunset. Stand upon the rocks at the bottom of the Mount of Mercy (Jabal ar-Rahmah); If not, then all of 'Arafah is a standing place. Facing the Qiblah, with raised hands, supplicate & also recite the talbiyah -

لَبَّيْكَ اللَّهُمَّ لَبَّيْك، لَبَّيْكَ لاَ شَرِيْكَ لَكَ لَبَّيْك

إِنَّ الْحَمْدَ وَ النِّعْمَةَ لَكَ وَ الْمُلْكُ لاَ شَرِيْكَ لَك

Here I am O Allaah, (in response to Your call), here I am. Here I am, You have no partner, here I am. Indeed all the Praise, Grace & Sovereignty belong to You. You have no partner.

It is encouraged to frequently recite the following -

لاَ إِلَهَ إِلاَّ اللهُ وَحْدَهُ لاَ شَرِيْكَ لَه، لَهُ الْمُلْك

وَ لَهُ الْحَمْد، وَ هُوَ عَلَى كُلِّ شَيْءٍ قَدِيْر

---

9 A place close to 'Arafah - there is now a Masjid there. If this is not possible, it is permissible to proceed to 'Arafah.

10 A place closer to 'Arafah than Namirah. If this is not possible, it is permissible to proceed to 'Arafah.

There is none truly worthy of worship except Al-laah alone, without partner. To Him belongs all Sovereignty & all Praise, & He is Omnipotent over all things.

- this is the best supplication to recite on this great day.

After sunset, calmly proceed to Muzdalifah.

Stay in Muzdalifah

Pray Maghrib & combine it with 'Ishaa in shortened form[11], after one Ad-haan & two Iqaamah's. Do not pray anything between these two prayers, nor pray anything after the Witr.

Go to sleep until Fajr.

4. 10th day of Dhul-Hijjah (Yawm an-Nahr)

Pray Fajr at its earliest time.

Calmly proceed to al-Mash'ar al-Haraam[12], ascend upon it. If not possible, then all of Muzdalifah is a standing place.

Facing Qiblah, praise Allaah by reciting -

All Praise is for Allaah.

---

11 Pray two Fard each for Zhuhr, 'Asr & 'Ishaa. Maghrib is not shortened, & remains three Fard. 'Ishaa to be followed by Witr.

12 A mountain in Muzdalifah.

- and proclaim the Greatness of Allaah by reciting -

اللهُ أَكْبَر

Allaah is the Greatest.

- then proclaim the Oneness of Allaah by reciting -

لاَ إِلَهَ إِلاَّ اللهُ

There is none truly worthy of worship except Al-laah.

- and finally, supplicate until the visibility of the yellow glow of the sun - before sunrise.

Before sunrise, calmly proceed to Minaa[13], reciting the talbiyah -

لَبَّيْكَ اللَّهُمَّ لَبَّيْكَ، لَبَّيْكَ لاَ شَرِيْكَ لَكَ لَبَّيْكَ

إِنَّ الْحَمْدَ وَ النِّعْمَةَ لَكَ وَ الْمُلْكُ لاَ شَرِيْكَ لَكَ

Here I am O Allaah, (in response to Your call), here I am. Here I am, You have no partner, here I am. Indeed all the Praise, Grace & Sovereignty belong to You. You have no partner.

---

13 If you pass through valley of Muhassar, then hurry through it.

Stoning

In Minaa, pick stones - seven required[14].

Between the time period of after sunrise until the night, calmly proceed to Jamarah al-'Aqabah al-Kubraa[15] for stoning. Facing Jamarah, with Makkah to your left & Minaa to your right, throw each of the seven stones at Jamarah reciting -

Allaah is the Greatest.

- after each throw.

After stoning, remove Ihraam, as all restrictions are now lifted except sexual intercourse.

If al-Hadee sacrificial ticket has been purchased, this is a permissible alternative, otherwise, calmly proceed to slaughter house in Minaa for sacrifice[16].

Sacrifice

Lie animal down on its left side, facing Qiblah. Place your right foot upon its right side. Upon slaughtering, recite -

بِسْمِ اللهِ وَ اللهُ أَكْبَر

اللَّهُمَّ إِنَّ هَذَا مِنْكَ وَ لَكَ اللَّهُمَّ تَقَبَّلْ مِنِّي

---

14 They must not be bigger than a chick-pea (approx. 1cm across).

15 The one nearest to Makkah.

16 Or any other appropriate place.

*In the name of Allaah, & Allaah is the Greatest. O
Allaah, it is from You & belongs to You. O Allaah,
accept this from me.*

As for a camel, approach it while it is standing facing Qiblah, and spear it
in the neck from below, making the same supplication, as above.

Shave Head

After slaughter, men: shave head - best, or cut hair equally from all over
head; women:cut one-third finger length of hair.

Calmly proceed to Makkah to perform Tawaaf al-Ifaadhah.

Tawaaf al-Ifaadhah

Upon entering al-Masjid al-Haraam with the right foot, recite -

اللَّهُمَّ صَلِّ عَلَى مُحَمَّدٍ وَ سَلِّم

اللَّهُمَّ افْتَحْ لِي أَبْوَابَ رَحْمَتِك

*O Allaah, send prayers & peace upon Muhammad,
O Allaah, open the doors of Your Mercy for me.*

No Ihraam required. Start at al-Hajar al-Aswad[17]. When beginning each

---

17 If possible, cling to area between the corner of al-Hajar al-Aswad & the door,
placing the chest, face & forearms upon this area.

circuit, make a sign with your right hand towards al-Hajar al-Aswad[18], & recite -

الله أَكْبَر

Allaah is the Greatest.

Walking at normal pace, make seven circuit's of Ka'bah[19]. During each circuit, whilst between ar-Rukn al-Yamaanee[20] & al-Hajar al-Aswad, recite -

{رَبَّنَا آتِنَا فِي الدُّنْيَا حَسَنَةً وَ فِي الآخِرَة

حَسَنَةً وَ قِنَا عَذَابَ النَّارِ}

Our Lord! Give us in this world that which is good & in the Hereafter that which is good, and save us from the torment of the Fire!

Then go behind Station of Ibraaheem and recite -

{وَاتَّخِذُوْا مِنْ مَّقَامِ إِبْرَاهِيْمَ مُصَلَّى}

And take the station of Ibraaheem as a place of prayer.

---

18 If possible, touch al-Hajar al-Aswad with the right hand & also kiss al-Hajar al-Aswad, then prostrate on it - this is best; if not, then touch it with the right hand then kiss the right hand; if not, simply make a sign towards it with the right hand.

19 There is no specific du'aa during the walk around the Ka'bah, apart from what has been mentioned for between ar-Rukn al-Yamaanee to al-Hajar al-Aswad. You can therefore recite the Qur.aan or any du'aa as you please.

20 If possible, touch ar-Rukn al-Yamaanee each time (but do not kiss it) - this is best; if not, then do not make any sign towards it.

Behind Station of Ibraaheem - if possible, otherwise anywhere within al-Masjid al-Haraam: Pray two rak'ah naafilah; In first rak'ah recite Soorah al-Kaafiroon & in second rakaah, Soorah al-Ikhlaas. Then go to Zam-Zam well & drink from it, then pour some water over head. Return to al-Hajar al-Aswad & make a sign with your right hand towards it for the last time[21], & recite -

الله أَكْبَر

Allaah is the Greatest.

Begin Sa'ee at as-Safaa. At foot of as-Safaa recite -

{إِنَّ الصَّفَا وَالْمَرْوَةَ مِنْ شَعَآئِرِ اللهِ فَمَنْ حَجَّ الْبَيْتَ أَوِ اعْتَمَرَ فَلاَ جُنَاحَ عَلَيْهِ أَنْ يَطَّوَّفَ بِهِمَا وَمَنْ تَطَوَّعَ خَيْراً فَإِنَّ اللهَ شَاكِرٌ عَلِيْمٌ}

نَبْدَأُ بِمَا بَدَأَ اللهُ بِه

Verily! as-Safaa & al-Marwah are of the Symbols of Allaah. So it is not a sin on him who performs Hajj or 'Umrah of the House to perform the Tawaaf between them. And whoever does good voluntarily, then verily, Allaah is All-Recogniser, All-Knower. We begin with what Allaah began with.

---

21 If possible, touch al-Hajar al-Aswad with the right hand & also kiss al-Hajar al-Aswad, then prostrate on it - this is best; if not, then touch it with the right hand then kiss the right hand; if not, simply make a sign towards it with the right hand.

Each time upon as-Safaa & al-Marwah facing Ka'bah, recite -

الله أَكْبَر، الله أَكْبَر، الله أَكْبَر

لاَ إِلَهَ إِلاَّ اللهُ وَحْدَهُ لاَ شَرِيْكَ لَه، لَهُ الْمُلْكُ وَ

لَهُ الْحَمْدُ يُحْيِي وَ يُمِيْتُ وَ هُوَ عَلَى كُلِّ شَيْءٍ

قَدِيْرٍ؛ لاَ إِلَهَ إِلاَّ اللهُ وَحْدَهُ لاَ شَرِيْكَ لَه، أَنْجَزَ

وَعْدَهُ وَ نَصَرَ عَبْدَهُ وَ هَزَمَ الأَحْزَابَ وَحْدَه

Allaah is the Greatest, Allaah is the Greatest, Al-laah is the Greatest. There is none truly worthy of worship except Allaah alone, without partner. To Him belongs all Sovereignty & all Praise. He alone gives life & causes death, He is Omnipotent over all things. There is none truly worthy of worship except Allaah alone, without partner. He has ful-filled His promise, & helped His slave, & He alone has defeated the confederates.

- three times, making du'aa after first & second recitation only.

Between the walk from as-Safaa to al-Marwah & al-Marwah to as-Safaa, it is permissable to recite -

رَبِّ اغْفِرْ وَارْحَم، إِنَّكَ أَنْتَ الأَعَزُّ الأَكْرَم

O Lord forgive me & have mercy, verily You are the Mightiest and Noblest.

226

Complete walk from as-Safaa to al-Marwah (one circuit), then al-Marwah to as-Safaa (second circuit) & continue for seven circuits, finishing at al-Marwah. Upon encountering green lights, men only - run from one light to other light.

Upon the completion of the Sa'ee, all restrictions are now lifted including sexual intercourse.

Upon leaving al-Masjid al-Haraam with the left foot, recite -

اللَّهُمَّ صَلِّ عَلَى مُحَمَّدٍ وَ سَلِّم

اللَّهُمَّ إِنِّي أَسْأَلُكَ مِنْ فَضْلِك

O Allaah, send prayers & peace upon Muhammad,
O Allaah, verily I ask You from Your Favour.

5. 11th, 12th and 13th days of Dhul-Hijjah (Ayyaam at-Tashreeq)

Stay in Minaa for stoning

From the time period between after Zawaal (sun at highest point - no shadow) until the night, stone all three Jamarahs.

Pick stones - twenty one required per day[22].

Facing first Jamarah, as-Sughraa[23], with Makkah to your left & Minaa to your right, throw each of the seven stones at Jamarah reciting -

---

22 They must not be bigger than a chick-pea (approx. 1cm across).

23 The one closest to Masjid al-Khayf.

الله أَكْبَر

Allaah is the Greatest.

- after each throw.

After stoning first Jamarah, face Qiblah (with first Jamarah to your right), raise hands & supplicate as you wish.

Then, calmly proceed to second Jamarah.

Facing second Jamarah, al-Wustaa[24], with Makkah to your left & Minaa to your right, throw each of the seven stones at Jamarah reciting -

الله أَكْبَر

Allaah is the Greatest.

- after each throw.

After stoning second Jamarah, face Qiblah (with second Jamarah to your right), raise hands & supplicate as you wish.

Then, calmly proceed to third Jamarah.

Facing third Jamarah, al-'Aqabah al-Kubraa[25], with Makkah to your left & Minaa to your right, throw each of the seven stones at Jamarah reciting

---

24 The middle one of the three.

25 The one nearest to Makkah.

اللهُ أَكْبَرُ

Allaah is the Greatest.

- after each throw.

After stoning third & final Jamarah, move onwards without supplicating.

After final stoning on 13th day of Dhul-Hijjah[26], calmly exit Minaa and proceed to Makkah.

Before final departure from Makkah, perform Tawaaf al-Wadaa' (Farewell Tawaaf) as your last act.

Tawaaf al-Wadaa'

Upon entering al-Masjid al-Haraam with the right foot, recite -

اللَّهُمَّ صَلِّ عَلَى مُحَمَّدٍ وَ سَلِّم
اللَّهُمَّ افْتَحْ لِي أَبْوَابَ رَحْمَتِك

O Allaah, send prayers & peace upon Muhammad,
O Allaah, open the doors of Your Mercy for me.

---

26 It is permissible to perform Tawaaf al-Wadaa' on 12th day of Dhul-Hijjah (as long as you leave Minaa before sunset), thus missing the recommended (but not compulsory) third day of stoning.

No Ihraam required. Start at al-Hajar al-Aswad[27]. When beginning each circuit, make a sign with your right hand towards al-Hajar al-Aswad[28], & recite -

اللهُ أَكْبَر

Allaah is the Greatest.

Walking at normal pace, make seven circuit's of Ka'bah[29]. During each circuit, whilst between ar-Rukn al-Yamaanee[30] and al-Hajar al-Aswad, recite -

{رَبَّنَا آتِنَا فِي الدُّنْيَا حَسَنَةً وَ فِي الآخِرَةِ
حَسَنَةً وَ قِنَا عَذَابَ النَّارِ}

Our Lord! Give us in this world that which is good
& in the Hereafter that which is good, and save us
from the torment of the Fire!

---

27 If possible, cling to area between the corner of al-Hajar al-Aswad & the door, placing the chest, face & forearms upon this area.

28 If possible, touch al-Hajar al-Aswad with the right hand & also kiss al-Hajar al-Aswad, then prostrate on it - this is best; if not, then touch it with the right hand then kiss the right hand; if not, simply make a sign towards it with the right hand.

29 There is no specific du'aa during the walk around the Ka'bah, apart from what has been mentioned for between ar-Rukn al-Yamaanee to al-Hajar al-Aswad. You can therefore recite the Qur.aan or any du'aa as you please.

30 If possible, touch ar-Rukn al-Yamaanee each time (but do not kiss it) - this is best; if not, then do not make any sign towards it.

Upon completion of Tawaaf al-Wadaa', you are free to depart to your home.

There is nothing further required of you from the rituals of Hajj.

Upon leaving al-Masjid al-Haraam with the left foot, recite -

اللَّهُمَّ صَلِّ عَلَى مُحَمَّدٍ وَ سَلِّم

اللَّهُمَّ إِنِّي أَسْأَلُكَ مِنْ فَضْلِك

O Allaah, send prayers & peace upon Muhammad,
O Allaah, verily I ask You from Your Favour.

Glossary of Arabic Terms

Aameen [آمِيْن]

Literally means, 'O Allaah! accept my/our invocation(s)'.

Aayah, pl. Aayaat [آية جـ آيات]

Sign, miracle, verse from the Noble Qur.aan.

Adhaan [أَذَان]

The call to prayer, pronounced vocally to indicate the time of prayer has entered.

Ahlus-Sunnah wal-Jamaa'ah [أَهْلُ السُّنَّة وَ الْجَمَاعَة]

Those who gather upon firm adherence to the Sunnah of the Prophet (sal-Allaahu 'alayhe wa sallam) and his Companions and follow their path in 'aqee-dah, speech and action, and thereby stand firm and upright upon this adherence and avoid innovations.

'Alayhis-Salaam [عَلَيْه السَّلام]

Literally means, 'Salutations be upon him'. This is to be said every time reference is made to any of the Messengers and Prophets of Allaah.

Al-'Asr [الْعَصْر]

Literally means, 'The Time'; It is also the name of the 103rd Soorah of the Qur.aan.

al-Hamdu Lillaah [الْحَمْدُ لله]
Literally means, 'All Praise is due to Allaah'.

Allaahu Akbar [الله أَكْبَر]
Literally means, 'Allaah is the Greatest'.

Allaahul-Musta'aan [الله الْمُسْتَعَان]
Literally means, 'Allaah is the One from Whom Assistance is sought'.

Ameer pl. Umaraa [أَمِير جـ أُمَرَاء]
A leader, one in charge.

Ameer al-Mu.mineen [أَمِير الْمُؤْمِنِيْن]
Commander of the Faithful, Commander of the Believers.

'Aqeedah, pl. 'Aqaa.id [عَقِيْدَة جـ عَقَائِد]
Creed, belief, doctrine.

'Arafah pl. 'Arafaat [عَرَفَة جـ عَرَفَات]
Open plain in the desert, approximately 12 miles outside Makkah. It is the place of gathering of the Hajj pilgrims on the 9th day of Dhul-Hijjah.

'Azza wa Jall [عَزَّ وَ جَلَّ]
Literally means, 'the Great and Almighty'; to whom belongs Might and Majesty.

Baara-kAllaahu Feek [بَارَكَ الله فِيْكَ]
Literally means, 'May Allaah bless you'.

Balaaghah [بَلاغَة]
Eloquence, good style, expressiveness, fluency.

al-Baqee al-Gharqad [الْبَقِيْع الْغَرْقَد]
The graveyard close to the Prophet's Masjid in Madeenah.

Daleel pl. Adillah [دَلِيْل جـ أَدِلَّة]
Proof, evidence, substantiation.

Da'wah, pl. Da'waat [دَعْوَة جـ دَعْوَات]
Missionary work to invite all people to worship Allaah as One, without associating any partners with Him; in short - Islaam.

Dhul-Hijjah [ذُوْ الْحِجَّة]
Twelfth month of the Islaamic Hijrah year.

Dhul-Qi'dah [ذُوْ الْقِعْدَة]
Eleventh month of the Islaamic Hijrah year.

Dhuhaa [ضُحَى]
The forenoon. Also the time for the voluntary prayer.

Du'aa pl. Ad'iyah [دُعَاء جـ أَدْعِيَة]
Invocation, supplication, prayer.

Eed al-Adh.haa [عِيْدُ الأَضْحَى]
The Feast of Sacrifice; The celebration held on the 10th through to the 13th days of Dhul-Hijjah.

Fajr [فَجْر]
Pre-dawn prayer; the first obligatory prayer of the day.

Fard Kifaayah [فَرْض كِفَايَة]
Collective obligation.

Fatwa, pl. Fataawa [فَتْوَى جـ فَتَاوَى]
Legal ruling based upon the Qur.aan and the Sunnah, passed by a Scholar in response to a question.

Fidyah [فِدْيَة]
Compensation, expiation, atonement, ransom. Redemption from the omission of a religious duty.

Firdows pl. Faraadees [فِرْدَوْس جـــ فَرَادِيْس]
Paradise, heaven. al-Firdows al-A'laa - the highest Heaven.

Fiqh [فِقْه]
Islaamic jurisprudence.

Fitnah, pl. Fitan [فِتْنَة جـــ فِتَن]
Test, affliction, civil strife, disorder, unrest, riot, turmoil, war, or satanic act.

Ghusl [غُسْل]
Major ritual ablution, washing oneself, bathing.

Haafiz, pl. Huffaaz [حَافظ جـــ حُفَّاظ]
One whose knowledge of hadéeth is more than that which he knows not; His comprehensive knowledge of hadeeth places him at a recognised level above the Muhaddith.

Hadeeth, pl. Ahaadeeth [حَدِيْث جـــ أَحَادِيْث]
Literally means, 'sayings' and could refer to the recorded quotes of anyone. Usually, it is the title given to the collection of recorded words, actions and tacit approvals of the Prophet Muhammad (sal-Allaahu 'alayhe wa sallam), which serve as an explanation of the meaning of the Noble Qur.aan.

al-Hajar al-Aswad [الْحَجَر الأَسْوَد]
The Black Stone attached to a corner of the Ka'bah, which marks the starting point of the tawaaf.

Hajj [حَجّ]
The 'major pilgrimage'. The once in a lifetime obligation (only if one possesses the means) of pilgrimage to Makkah; made up of specified rites performed between the 8th to the 13th day of Dhul-Hijjah (the twelfth month of the Islaamic Hijrah year). It is one of the five pillars of Islaam.

Halaal [حَلال]
Lawful, legal, licit, allowed, allowable, permissible, permitted.

Hanafee, pl. Hanafiyyah / Ahnaaf [أَحْنَاف / حَنَفِيَّة ـــجـ حَنَفِيّ]

An adherent to, or a student of the School of Islaamic Jurisprudence which is based upon the teachings of Abu Haneefah Nu'maan ibn Thaabit ibn Zootaa ibn Marzubaan (died in Baghdad 148 Hijree / 767 AD).

Hanbalee, pl. Hanaabilah [حَنَابِلَة ـــجـ حَنْبَلِي]

An adherent to, or a student of the School of Islaamic Jurisprudence which is based upon the teachings of Abu 'Abdullaah Ahmad ibn Muhammad ibn Hanbal ash-Shaybaanee (died in Baghdad 241 Hijree / 855 AD).

Haraam [حَرَام]

Unlawful, illegal, illicit, illegitimate, forbidden, prohibited, banned, taboo, disallowed, barred.

Haram [حَرَم]

Holy sanctuary, sacred precinct. The term referred to the sacred precinct of Makkah [الْحَرَم الْمَكِّيّ] and Madeenah [الْحَرَم الْمَدَنِيّ].

Hijr Ismaa'eel [حِجْرُ إِسْمَاعِيْل]

The semi-circle walled enclosure, adjacent to the Ka'bah.

Hijrah [هِجْرَة]

Emigration, expatriation, exodus, immigration (to), migration. Prophet Muhammad's (sal-Allaahu 'alahe wa sallam) migration from Makkah to Madeenah marks the beginning of the Islaamic Hijrah calendar.

Hijree [هِجْري]

The term referred to a year of the Islaamic Hijrah calendar.

'Ibaadah [عَبَادَة]

Act of worship, religious observances, forms of worship, devotions.

'Iddah [عِدَّة]

A woman's prescribed waiting period after her divorce or the death of her husband.

Ifraad [إِفْرَاد]

The performing of hajj without 'umrah.

Ihraam [إِحْرَام]

A state of ritual consecration for Hajj or 'Umrah. A state in which the Muslim is prohibited from doing some permissible things because of devotion to worship.

Ihsaan [إِحْسَان]

Doing good, acting in an upright manner.

Imaam, pl. A.immah [إِمَام جـــ أَئِمَّة]

A distinguished and recognised scholar; Generally recognised to be at a level above the 'Allaamah, and often referred to as a Mujaddid (reformer and reviver of the religion). Also used to refer to the one who leads the prayer.

Inshaa.-Allaah [إِنْ شَاءَ الله]

Literally means, 'if Allaah wills'.

I'raab [إِعْرَاب]

Arabic grammar term denoting the analysis of a word in a sentence and, where applicable, any change affected upon it by a preceding word resulting in a modification/change reaching the end of the word.

'Ishaa [عِشَاء]

Night prayer; the last obligatory prayer of the day.

Islaam [إِسْلام]

Submission, surrender, obedience to the Will of Allaah.

Izaar [إِزَار]

An unstitched piece of waist wrapped cloth; a wraparound.

Jamarah pl. Jamaraat [جَمَرَة جـــ جَمَرَات]

Stoning pillar. Jamarah al-'Aqabah al-Kubraa is the closest of the three stoning pillars to Makkah, and Jamarah al-Wustaa is the middle one, and Jamarah as-Sughraa is the smallest one.

Jam'u Taqdeem [جَمْعُ تَقْدِيْم]

The combining of two prayers, i.e. the Zhuhr with the 'Asr at the time of Zhuhr, or the Maghrib with the 'Ishaa at the time of Maghrib.

Janaabah [جَنَابَة]

Major ritual impurity, grave impurity, ceremonial impurity, the greater incident.

Jihaad [جهَاد]

To strive hard, or to fight to defend one's life, property, freedom, and religion. It can also refer to an attempt to free other people from oppression and tyranny. Importantly, Islaam strongly opposes the kidnapping, terrorising, or hijacking of civilians, even during war.

Jumaada al-Aakhir / ath-Thaanee [جُمَادى الآخِر / الثَّانِي]

Sixth month of the Islaamic Hijrah year.

Jumu'ah [جُمُعَة]

The Friday prayer performed in jamaa'ah after the khutbah. This is in place of the Salaat az-Zhuhr.

Kaafir, pl. Kaafiroon / Kuffaar / Kafarah

[كَافِر جـ كَافِرُوْن / كُفَّار / كَفَرَة]

Disbeliever, infidel, non-believer, one who disbelieves, unbelieveing person, one who rejects (faith), one who denies.

Ka'bah [كَعْبَة]

The cubic stone building at the centre of al-Masjid al-Haraam in Makkah, towards which the Muslims turn five-times daily for prayers. It is also referred to as the House of Allaah.

Khateeb pl. Khutabaa [خَطِيْب جـ خُطَبَاء]

A public speaker, orator; Popularly used to refer to the one who delivers the Friday khutbah.

Khutbah, pl. Khutab [خُطْبَة جـ خُطَب]

A public sermon, address, speech.

Kiswah [كِسْوَة]
Covering cloth of the Ka'bah.

Kufr [كُفْر]
Disbelief, infidelity.

Laa ilaaha il-Allaah [لاَ إِلَهَ إِلاَّ الله]
Literally means, 'There is none truly worthy of worship except Allaah.'

Maalikee, pl. Maalikiyyah [مَالِكِيّ جـ مَالِكِيَّة]
An adherent to, or a student of the School of Islaamic Jurisprudence which is based upon the teachings of Abu 'Abdullaah Maalik ibn Anas ibn Maalik ibn 'Amr al-Asbahi (died in Madeenah 179 Hijree / 795 AD).

Madhhab, pl. Madhaahib [مَذْهَب جـ مّذَاهِب]
School, school of Islaamic jurisprudence, school of religious law, doctrine, persuasion, sect, way, manner.

Maghrib [مَغْرِب]
After sunset prayer; the fourth obligatory prayer of the day.

Mahram [مَحْرَم]
An unmarriageable male chaperone; A husband or a near male relative, such as a father, brother or son - who is eternally prohibited from marrying a certain woman.

Maqaam Ibraaheem [مَقَام إِبْرَاهِيْم]
The place where Prophet Ibraheem ('alayhis-salaam) stood in prayer whilst the Ka'bah was being built.

al-Marwah [الْمَرْوَة]
The second of the two mounts neighbouring to the east of al-Masjid al-Haraam. It is required to perform the sa'ee between the two mounts seven times, (ending at al-Marwah) during the Hajj and the 'Umrah.

Mas'aa [مَسْعًى]

The walkway between the Mounts of as-Safaa and al-Marwah, where the sa'ee is performed.

al-Mash'ar al-Haraam [الْمَشْعَر الْحَرَام]

Sacred Mount, Supplication Hill. The pilgrimage station at Muzdalifah.

Masjid, pl. Masaajid [مَسْجِد جـ مَسَاجِد]

The Muslim's place of worship.

al-Masjid al-Haraam [الْمَسْجِد الْحَرَام]

'The Grand Masjid' in Makkah; which is the holiest masjid in Islaam.

al-Masjid an-Nabawee [الْمَسْجِد النَّبَوِي]

'The Prophet's Masjid' in Madeenah; which is the second holiest masjid in Islaam.

Meeqaat pl. Mawaaqeet [مِيْقَات جـ مَوَاقِيْت]

Legally appointed place for assuming the state of ihraam for Hajj and 'Umrah.

Mihraab [مِحْرَاب]

Prayer niche. The place where the imaam stands to lead the prayer in the masjid.

Minbar, pl. Manaabir [مِنْبَر جـ مَنَابِر]

Pulpit, platform, stand, rostrum,

Muhaddith, pl. Muhaddithoon [مُحَدِّث جـ مُحَدِّثُوْن]

A distinguished scholar of hadeeth. His level of knowledge is lesser than that of the Haafiz.

Mufti [مُفْتِي]

Interpreter or expounder of the Sharee'ah; deliverer of legal religious verdicts.

Muharram [مُحَرَّم]

First month of the Islaamic Hijrah year.

240

Muhrim [مُحْرِم]

One who has assumed the state of ihraam.

Muh.sar [مُحْصَر]

One who is prevented from performing the hajj or the 'umrah.

Mujaahid, pl. Mujaahidoon [مُجَاهِدُوْن ــ جـ مُجَاهِد]

Struggler; one engaged in jihaad.

Musannaf [مُصَنَّف]

A comprehensive collection of ahaadeeth in which the traditions are assembled and arranged in various 'books' or 'chapters', each dealing with a particular topic. To this class belong the Muwatta of Imaam Maalik, the Saheeh of Muslim, and similar works.

Musnad [مُسْنَد]

A collection of traditions listing the names of the Companions in alphabetical order. The most important and exhaustive of all the musnad works available is that of Imaam Ahmad ibn Hanbal.

Mustadrak [مُسْتَدْرَك]

A collection of traditions which the compiler, having accepted the conditions laid down by a previous compiler, collects together such other traditions as fulfil those conditions and were missed by his perdecessor. To this class belongs the Mustadrak of al-Haakim an-Neesaabooree, who assembled a large number of ahaadeeth which fulfilled the stringent conditions laid down by al-Bukhaaree and Muslim, but were not included in their Saheeh compilations.

Naafilah, pl. Nawaafil [نَوَافل ــ جـ نَافِلَة]

Voluntary act of worship.

Nahr, Day of [يَوْم النَّحْر]

The 10th day of Dhul-Hijjah, the day of 'Eed al-Adh.haa, the day of sacrifice / slaughter.

Niqaab [نِقَاب]

Veil; A fine light cloth covering worn by women - used to drop over the face in the presence of non-mahram men.

Qiblah [قِبْلَة]

Direction of prayer. The direction towards the Ka'bah in al-Masjid al-Haraam in Makkah.

Qiraan [قِرَان]

The combining of hajj with 'umrah during the legislated months of hajj, whilst maintaining the same single state of ihraam.

Qur.aan [قُرْآن]

Compiled divine revelations from Allaah to Prophet Muhammad; The Holy Book of the Muslims.

Radhi-yAllaahu 'anhu / 'anhaa / 'anhumaa / 'anhum

[رَضِيَ اللهُ عَنْهُ / عَنْهَا / عَنْهُمَا / عَنْهُمْ]

Literally means, 'May Allaah be pleased with him / her / with the two of them / with them'.

Rahima-hullaah / hallaah / humullaah

[رَحِمَهُ / رَحِمَهَا / رَحِمَهُمُ الله]

Literally means, 'May Allaah have mercy upon him / her / upon them'.

Rajab [رَجَب]

Seventh month of the Islaamic Hijrah year.

Rak'ah pl. Raka'aat [رَكْعَة جــ رَكَعَات]

A single unit of prayer consisting of the standing, bowing and prostrating positions.

Ramadhaan [رَمَضَان]

Ninth month of the Islaamic Hijrah year. Fasting has been prescribed from dawn til dusk for the duration of this month.

Ribaa [رِبَا]

Interest, usury. It is of two types:

(i) Ribaa Nissee.a, ie interest on lent money;

(ii) Ribaa Fadhl, ie taking a superior thing of the same kind of goods by giving more of the same kind of goods of inferior quality, eg dates of superior quality for dates of inferior quality in greater amount. Islaam strictly forbids all types of usury.

Ridaa [رِدَاء]

An unstitched piece of torso wrapped cloth; a wraparound.

Saa' [صَاع]

A Saa' is equal to four (4) Mudd, and one (1) Mudd is equal to the amount held by cupping the two hands together. It is a measure by volume not by weight.

Sadaqah pl. Sadaqaat [صَدَقَات ــج صَدَقَة]

A voluntary gift of charity.

Sa'ee [سَعِي]

Walking seven times between the mountains of Safaa and Marwa during the Hajj and the 'Umrah.

as-Safaa [الصَّفَا]

The first of the two mounts neighbouring to the east of al-Masjid al-Haraam. It is required to perform the sa'ee between the two mounts seven times, (beginning at as-Safaa) during the Hajj and the 'Umrah.

Saheeh, pl. Sihaah [صِحَاح ــج صَحِيْح]

Authentic, correct.

as-Salaam 'Alaykum [السَّلَام عَلَيْكُم]

Literally means, 'peace be upon you'. It is the expression used by Muslims to greet each other.

Sal-Allaahu 'Alayhe wa Sallam [صَلَّى الله عَلَيْهِ وَ سَلَّم]
Literally means, 'May Allaah send prayers and salutations upon him'. This is to be said every time reference is made to the final Messenger of Allaah, Muhammad.

Salaah, pl. Salawaat [صَلاة جـ صَلَوَات]
Term referred to specific supplications and actions, correctly understood as prayers. The Muslims are required to perform five daily prayers. It is one of the five pillars of Islaam.

Salaatul Jamaa'ah [صَلاةُ الْجَمَاعَة]
The congregational prayer.

Salaf, pl. Aslaaf [سَلَف جـ أَسْلاَف]
The first three generations of Muslims. Popularly referred to as 'as-Salaf as-Saalih' [السَّلَفُ الصَّلِح] - the pious predecessors.

Shaafi'ee, pl. Shaafi'iyyah [شَافِعِيّ جـ شَافِعِيَّة]
An adherent to, or a student of the School of Islaamic Jurisprudence which is based upon the teachings of Abu 'Abdullaah Muhammad ibn Idrees ash-Shaafi'ee (died in Fustat, Egypt 204 Hijree / 820 AD).

Sha'baan [شَعْبَان]
Eighth month of the Islaamic Hijrah year.

Sharee'ah, pl. Sharaa.i' [شَرِيْعَة جـ شَرَائِع]
The Islaamic Law, in particular, what is stated in the texts of the Qur.aan and the Sunnah.

Shawwaal [شَوَّال]
Tenth month of the Islaamic Hijrah year.

Shaykh, pl. Shuyookh, Mashaa.ikh, Mashaayikh
[شَيْخ جـ شُيُوْخ / مَشَائِخ / مَشَايِخ]
Correctly referred to as a religious scholar; however, it is also referred to one who is elderly.

Shirk [شِرْك]
Associating partners in worship with Allaah.

Soorah, pl. Suwar [سُوْرَة جـ سُوَر]
Chapter; one of the 114 chapters of the Noble Qur.aan.

Subhaanahu wa Ta'aala [سُبْحَانَهُ وَ تَعَالَى]
Literally means, 'How perfect He is, the Almighty'; Complete meaning: 'I exalt Him and elevate Him above having any defects or deficiencies'.

Sujood / Sajdah, pl. Sajadaat [سُجُوْد / سَجْدَة جـ سَجَدَات]
The prostration posture in salaah.

Sunnah, pl. Sunan [سُنَّة جـ سُنَن]
Way, mode, manner; correctly referred to as the words, actions and tacit approvals of the Prophet Muhammad (sal-Allaahu 'alayhe wa sallam), which serve as an explanation of the meaning of the Noble Qur.aan.

Tafseer, pl. Tafaaseer [تَفْسِيْر جـ تَفَاسِيْر]
Commentary, exegesis, explanation.

Tahajjud [تَهَجُّد]
Supererogatory night prayer - best performed during the last third of the night.

Tahiyyatul-Masjid [تَحِيَّةُ الْمَسْجِد]
The two rak'ah prayer offered promptly upon entering the masjid, before sitting down.

Tajweed [تَجْوِيْد]
Rules governing the correct recitation of the Qur.aan.

Takbeer pl. Takbeeraat [تَكْبِيْر جـ تَكْبِيْرَات]
The proclamation of 'Allaahu Akbar'.

Talbiyah [تَلْبِيَة]

Answering the call to pilgrimage. Pronouncing one's coming to Allaah in obedience, saying 'Here I am [in response to Your call Allaah] performing hajj / 'umrah'.

Tamattu' [تَمَتُّع]

The combining of hajj with 'umrah during the legislated months of hajj, in two separate states of ihraam; one for 'umrah and then one for hajj.

Taraaweeh [تَرَاوِيح]

Voluntary prayers offered after the 'Ishaa prayer during the nights of Ramadhaan. These may be performed individually or in congregation.

Tarwiyyah, Day of [يَوْم التَّرْوِيَة]

The 8th day of Dhul-Hijjah.

Tashreeq, Days of [أَيَّام التَّشْرِيق]

The 11th, 12th and 13th days of Dhul-Hijjah.

Tasleem [تَسْلِيْم]

The salutation of 'as-salaam 'alaykum wa rahmatullaah' pronounced upon completing the salaah.

Tawaaf [طَوَاف]

Circumambulation of the Ka'bah.

Tawaaf al-Ifaadhah [طَوَاف الإِفَاضَة]

Circumambulation of the Ka'bah after returning from Muzdalifah.

Tawaaf al-Wadaa' [طَوَاف الإِفَاضَة]

Circumambulation of the Ka'bah upon departing from Makkah.

Towfeeq [تَوْفِيْق]

Success and good fortune granted by Allaah.

Udh.hiyah, pl. Adhaahee [أُضْحِيَة جـ أَضَاحِي]

Animal sacrifice.

'Umrah [عُمْرَة]
The 'minor pilgrimage'. It has fewer rites than the 'major pilgrimage' (Hajj). In general, it may be performed at any time of the year.

Usool ad-Deen [أُصُوْل الدِّيْن]
Principles of the religion.

Usool al-Fiqh [أُصُوْل الْفِقْه]
Principles of Islaamic Jurisprudence.

Waajib [وَاجب]
Obligatory, mandatory, compulsory.

Wudhoo [وُضُوْء]
Ablution, minor ritual ablution, washing oneself in a prescribed manner in preparation for salaah or other acts of worship.

Za'faraan [زَعْفَرَان]
Saffron. Used to color foods and as a cooking spice and dyestuff.

Zakaah, pl. Zakawaat [زَكَاة جـ زَكَوَات]
The alms tax deducted from the Muslims wealth at a rate of 2.5%, and distributed to the poor and needy. It is one of the five pillars of Islaam.

Zam Zam [زَمْزَم]
The holy water well located within al-Masjid al-Haraam, close to the Ka'bah. The Prophet (sal-Allaahu 'alayhe wa sallam) said: *«Zam Zam water is for what it is drunk for»*.

Zawaal [زَوَال]
Noon, midday, when the Sun above is at its highest point, casting no shadow.

Zhuhr [ظُهَر]
After noon prayer; the second obligatory prayer of the day.

Notes